EXPLORING EUCHARIST

Donal Harrington

Exploring Eucharist

THOUGHTS, MEDITATIONS, IDEAS

the columba press

First published in 2007 by
the columba press
55A Spruce Avenue, Stillorgan Industrial Park,
Blackrock, Co Dublin

Cover by Bill Bolger
Origination by The Columba Press
Printed in Ireland by ColourBooks Ltd, Dublin

ISBN 978 1 85607 588 6

Table of Contents

*Each of these sections begins with its own more detailed
table of contents.*

Introduction

Some people wonder what can be done to get younger people back to Mass. They are concerned about how to communicate to them what they are missing. They want to instil interest and appreciation. They may also bemoan what they perceive as a lack of responsibility in those who do not take part.

Other people wonder what can be done to make the Mass more interesting. Their concern is how to relieve the boredom, the monotony, the lethargy in the liturgy. They want to inject the kind of life that would make it more attractive. They suspect that, were they themselves younger again, they would be the ones not coming.

There is empirical evidence that people today (and more than we might imagine) will come to Mass when the Mass is interesting and enjoyable. We have only to look at many family Masses, folk Masses, youth Masses, gospel Masses, as well as many more traditional Masses. Where there is a commitment to quality, allied to an energy of faith, things happen.

It isn't about putting on a show in order to draw people in – just as it isn't about beating people back into something they gave up. Essentially, though it sounds odd, it's about the people who still go to Mass. It's about deepening and transforming their experience – which, to be honest, more often than not leaves a lot to be desired. There is a lot of new life in the celebration of the Eucharist today. But there is also a lot of mediocrity and deadness.

This book is about the people who do go, however regularly or sporadically, and what they make of what is going on at Mass. Its premise is that, if we who go can enrich our understanding, that will feed into transforming our celebration. That in turn will be found attractive, nourishing and challenging by other people not currently participating.

Section one seeks to refresh our sense of the familiar words we say each week. Section two goes down different paths, to see what the Eucharist looks like from different angles. Section three is a more systematic elaboration of the meaning of the main parts of the Mass, with practical suggestions for celebrating them.

I am grateful for the experiences that originated this book – particularly the liturgy courses I presented in the parishes of Dundrum, Beaumont and Holy Redeemer Bray; as well as a series of reflections composed for the weekly newsletter in Dundrum parish.

Familiar Phrases

This section contains brief meditations on the following familiar words
which we hear or say during our celebration of the Eucharist:

In the name of the Father and of the Son and of the Holy Spirit.

The sign of the cross – the sign of the Trinity.
We do it, hardly noticing sometimes,
a reflex when we hear bad news,
or when a funeral passes
or passing a church.

And yet it is full of mystery:
the Trinity – the glorious, almighty, resplendent God;
and the Cross – inglorious, powerless, ignominious;
totally giving, generous, self-emptying God.

As I make the sign of the cross,
I bless the Father, who gives me life;
I bless the Son, who shows me the way;
I bless the Spirit, encouraging my spirit.

And I pray:
may this Trinity live in me
and help me to be giving, generous, self-emptying –
a sign of the cross.

The Lord be with you
and also with you.

'Dia dhuit' –
we used to greet each other like this.
Now it's only at Mass.
But isn't it a beautiful way to be greeted?

Feel yourself being spoken to with these words,
'The Lord be with you';
and feel it happening!

The Lord *is* with me – I am safe,
I need not be anxious or afraid,
I can continue – I can make a difference.

And also with *you*!
I make time and space to be amazed
that the Lord is with you –
that you are an epiphany of divine beauty –
and I salute you.

The grace of our Lord Jesus Christ
and the love of God
and the fellowship of the Holy Spirit

Grace, love, fellowship –
that each of us may carry this blessed trinity
in our hearts and minds.

When we carry this trinity with us,
we receive the gifts of faith, of hope and of love –
the 'interior trinity'.

The love of God created us
and constantly holds us in being;
appreciating this is the gift of faith.

The grace of our Lord Jesus Christ enlightens our minds
and shows us how to live;
this is the gift of love.

The fellowship of the Holy Spirit
accompanying us on life's path,
encouraging, sustaining, forgiving;
forever renewing its gift of hope.

I look within –
I feel the gifts of faith, hope and love welling up,
and I know that your life, Lord, is my life
and that my life is your life.

I confess to almighty God

There are three kinds of confession
that happen during the Eucharist.

Confession of faith is the Creed
when together we profess our belief in God,
the Trinity of Father, Son and Spirit,
and in the Church, the temple of God's Spirit.

Confession of thanks and praise
is what 'Eucharist' is all about,
and the Eucharistic prayer in particular.

Confession of sins happens at the start of Mass
when together we acknowledge that we are sinners
in need of God's mercy.

When we say 'I confess' we speak with hope
for our confession of sins arises from
our confession of who God is
and our thanks for what God does for us.

Lord, we believe in you, Father, Son and Spirit;
we praise and thank you for your loving kindness;
and we rejoice in your forgiveness as we say,
'I confess to almighty God …'

Christ have mercy
May almighty God have mercy on us

The word 'mercy' suggests asking pardon
from one who is all-powerful,
or clemency, when one has been proven guilty.

So I can only say the words 'have mercy on me'
when I am aware of being guilty
and when I am aware of myself speaking to one
who is far greater than I am.

But when I say 'Christ have mercy'
there is another element
besides 'guilty' and 'greater than I'.
It is that I know the character of the one whom I implore.

Not an implacable judge from whom little can be expected,
nor an unfeeling, distant authority.
But one who has a profound compassion for me
in my fragility
and a true grasp of my deep desire,
and a sense of who I can be
that is far greater than my own.

May all who call on the Lord have a deep realisation
that their lives are bathed in inexhaustible compassion.

Glory to God in the highest
We worship you, we give you thanks, we praise you for your glory

(This prayer of praise follows naturally
when the previous prayer is felt to be
a celebration of God's forgiveness
rather than a mournful reminder of guilt.)

When I say 'Glory to God'
I am saying that I adore you,
you who alone are God.

Although we use the word 'adore' loosely –
of another person, or a painting, or fine food –
there is only one fitting object of our adoration,
that is You.

To glorify you is to express the heart
of the relationship between us;
that I am creature and you are creator,
that I am searching and you are my salvation.

And when I glorify and adore you,
I am most free.
I am letting my spirit soar,
not asking for anything,
nor grovelling or cajoling or doing business,
but simply proclaiming who you are.

We ask this through Christ our Lord

Why do we make our prayers 'through' Christ,
'in the name of Jesus'?
Why do we not speak directly to God?

Perhaps it is because he is where humanity and divinity are one,
the point of intersection
where each flows into the other
through him.

> 'It is Christ Jesus who died, yes, who was raised,
> who is at the right hand of God,
> who indeed intercedes for us.' (*Romans 8:34*)

Perhaps it is because he is praying for us all the time
and our occasional prayers are our tuning into
his constant prayer for us.

All his life was a prayer, accepted by the Father.
His death and resurrection are our salvation;
our reconciliation, the end of isolation and estrangement;
the pledge to us of undying love.
He is all our prayers asked and answered.

We make our prayer through him
for him to make it part of his prayer
and for it to share in his victory.

'Father, I am praying for those whom you gave me ...'
(*John 17:9*)

A reading from …
This is the word of the Lord

'A reading from …' sounds unremarkable.
But this is not any 'word'
like a railway station announcement or newspaper headline.
It is God's word, the word of the One who said:

> 'For as the rain and snow come down from heaven
> and do not return there until they have watered the earth …
> so shall my word be that goes out from my mouth;
> it shall not return to me empty,
> but it shall accomplish that which I purpose
> and succeed in the thing for which I sent it.' *(Isaiah 55:10-11)*

This Word is an *event*,
no less than consecration –
an encounter with God speaking to me
with a word for me.

It has the power to connect with me –
to light up my life,
to transform my view,
to give me a handle on things –

if I can but connect with it,
by opening my heart,
by awaiting its grace
and placing myself in the shadow of its power.

May my heart be rich soil, ready and receptive,
where the gospel grows strong roots and bears rich fruit.

We believe in one God …

This is the second 'confession' in the Mass –
the confession of what we believe.

The Creed is not a matter-of-fact statement
of *what* we believe about 'God'.
We are confessing the *who* behind the name –
revealed to us by the self-disclosure
of One whom we could never comprehend.

The 'Father' who created us and holds us in being;
the 'Son' in whom God takes on a face we can recognise;
the 'Spirit', the living presence of this God
who has come incredibly close to us in Jesus.

The *who* behind the name –
the God who enters into intimacy with us;
the God who invites us to participate
in a breath-taking exchange of love.

'We believe' –
not a statement of beliefs or doctrines about 'God',
but an utterance from the heart
of what we have come to know
about the face behind the name.

Lord hear us
Lord hear our prayer

We don't say 'Hear me, hear my prayer'
but 'Lord hear *us*, hear *our* prayer'.
Does prayer carry more power when plural?

'If two of you agree on earth about anything you ask,
it will done for you by my Father in heaven' *(Matthew 18:19).*
In Jesus' eyes, there is something special
about the prayer we make together.

The 'prayer of the faithful' is just that.
It takes us beyond personal needs and wants;
it is more than the preferences of any individual.
It articulates the prayer of all of us together
for ourselves
for other members of the body of Christ
for all who share a common humanity.

And when we say 'Lord hear us'
it's not as if God might not be listening
(it might well be about increasing *our* awareness and desire).
When we ask the Lord to hear us,
when we pray with one heart, as one body,
the Spirit 'hears' our prayer into the heart of God.

Blessed are you, Lord God of all creation

For the goodness of life,
for the wonder of the world,
for the miracle of love,
for the beauty of the seasons,
for the renewal of hope,
we bless you Lord.

So often we ask for almighty God to bless us,
but here the blessing is in the other direction.
We bless you, creator and saviour God –
for the goodness of your creation
and for the great goodness of your creating us.

We bless you, who have blessed us.
We bless you – and await your blessing.

Pray that our sacrifice may be acceptable
to God the almighty Father

The sacrifice of the Mass ... Jesus' sacrifice on the altar ...
There is something else here also.
We have just brought our gifts, bread and wine,
and now we say, may 'our' sacrifice be acceptable.

Bread and wine represent *us*.
We bring ourselves to the table of the Lord.
Yet we rarely think of this –
the sacrifice of Calvary, yes;
the sacrifice of the altar, yes;
but the sacrifice of ourselves?

> 'I appeal to you to present your bodies
> as a living sacrifice,
> holy and acceptable to God,
> which is your spiritual worship.' *(Romans 12:1)*

May our lives be a spiritual sacrifice to God,
offered in Jesus' own spirit, with single-minded trust.

May our offering of ourselves be from a pure heart,
genuinely meant,
seriously intended,
acceptable to God –
ready material for divine transformation.

Lift up your hearts

How is your heart as you hear these words?
Are you down-hearted, heavy-hearted, broken-hearted?
Are you feeling heartened, or 'hale and hearty'?
Are you good-hearted, great-hearted, open-hearted?
Is your heart in the right place?
What heartfelt feelings emanate from within you?

The Lord says, 'Lift up your heart.'
Why?
Because if you lift up your heart
your heart will see something more
than it can see at present –
it will see into the heart of God,
opened for us, broken for us.

The Lord says, 'Lift up your heart.'
Why?
Because this is the time of grace.
Lift up your heart
and your spirits will be uplifted.

May the celebration of the Eucharist
be an uplifting experience for all;
may it give us new heart for living.

It is right to give him thanks and praise

The third 'confession' of our Mass,
after the confession of sin and the confession of faith –
this is the confession of thanks and praise.
('Eucharist' means giving thanks.)

'Thanks be to God' – an everyday phrase
but its meaning is that it is an enduring attitude –
we thank God for everything and in everything.

If we were to thank and praise God
only in good times and only for good things,
that would be to paint God as whimsical –
'If I thank God now, I may be so lucky again.'

But 'in everything God works for the good' *(Romans 8:28)*.
Every situation, however terrible or wonderful,
can be a moment of grace and blessing.
If grace is working on the Cross,
then grace works in everything.

So, in every situation, I await with confidence
the grace that is waiting to be revealed.
Grace is the constant presence in our lives
and this is why
'It is right to give him thanks and praise.'

Holy, holy, holy

We call God 'holy' – what could that mean?
Is it like when we call people holy?
Very religious, deeply prayerful, always going to church?

God's holiness is God's wonder
breath-taking and intimate;
God's holiness is God's 'godness'
calling for awe and veneration;
God's holiness is God's glory
uniquely deserving of adoration.

So, not for the first time in the Mass,
we are in the mode most becoming to us as creatures –
the mode of honouring and adoring God –
for no other reason than that God is God,
greater than all goodness and truth and beauty.

Well, not quite 'for no other reason';
we say 'holy' also because God has blessed us in Christ
with a touch of divinity;
and so we say,
'Blessed is he who comes in the name of the Lord,
Hosanna in the highest.'

Take this, all of you, and eat it
this is my body
Take this, all of you, and drink from it
this is the cup of my blood

The priest is facing us – it is Jesus we see.
The priest speaks to us – it is Jesus we hear.
Seeing and hearing Jesus, we see and hear God –
his body given for us
his blood shed for us –
a surprising God, at my feet
a humble God, washing my feet.

How often it happens every day
that one person is bread for another
that one person pours themselves out for another –
parent for child, friend for friend –
that one person is gift for another …

and to think that this is God.

Do this in memory of me

Each year a group of friends gather for a meal,
around the anniversary of the death some years earlier
of one of their number.
There is no difficulty assembling the group.
Everything else is put aside.
Everybody turns up.

They gather to remember.
In remembering, they stay faithful.
Their friend continues to mean much to them.
Remembering keeps something alive.
Their friend goes on living,
in their hearts and minds,
in their courage and conscience.

As we obey the Lord's command,
may our remembering
keep us in touch with who he is
and who we are.

Let us proclaim the mystery of faith

How do I 'proclaim' and not just 'repeat' or 'say' the words?

Think about the words themselves:

> *'Dying you destroyed our death, rising you restored our life.'*
> *'We proclaim your death, Lord Jesus, until you come in glory.'*
> *'Lord, by your cross and resurrection you have set us free.'*
> *'Christ has died, Christ is risen, Christ will come again.'*

These words are salvation! They are good news.
They embody the reality of what we are –
words to be declared and not just repeated.

Our hearts proclaim these words, not just our mouths.
'If you confess with your lips that Jesus is Lord
and believe in your heart
that God raised him from the dead
you will be saved.' *(Romans 10:9)*

Our lives proclaim these words, not just our hearts.
As Francis of Assisi put it:
'Every Christian is called to proclaim the good news
and if necessary, to use words.'

That our lives may proclaim what our hearts and lips profess;
that gospel joy and hope might radiate out from us.

Through him, with him and in him,
in the unity of the Holy Spirit,
all glory and honour is yours, almighty Father

Christians don't just pray to God.
They always pray through, with and in Christ.
We cannot pray to God apart from Christ,
as if they were two independent addressees.

That is how much Christ means to us;
God is in him in such a way
and so completely
that we can only pray to God
through him, with him and in him.

As we pray, we find ourselves caught up
in Jesus' own orientation to God –
his single-minded devotion,
his steadfast dedication.

We are caught up in his Last Supper prayer of thanks.
We join in his perfect prayer
and allow God's honour and glory
to be the shape and the sense
of all our desires.

May all that we do be done for the greater glory of God;
may the lives we lead be a song of praise to God.

Our Father ...

We recall what is so amazing about these words –
that they come from the mouth of the Master.
This sets it apart from any other prayer
by putting us in such direct contact with him.

Not just that;
the prayer is Jesus' response to one of his disciples
(having seen Jesus praying)
asking him to teach them to pray.

Today, we are those disciples.
So these words are not just from his mouth;
he is also addressing them especially to us,
giving them specifically to us, today, to say –
a personalised communication.

Not just that;
it is reasonable to suppose that the words reflect
the prayer that Jesus himself offered to the Father.

So we are also praying his prayer,
we are alongside him, communing with the Father –
a fitting way into the 'communion' part of the Mass.

All of this makes sacred
the prayer's every word and sentiment,
meant to sink into our imagination,
to mould our sense of self,
to shape our attitudes and action.

Deliver us, Lord, from every evil
Keep us free from sin and protect us from all anxiety

'Deliver us – keep us free – protect us'.
We are *already* delivered, freed, protected
by what God has done in Jesus.
But Eucharist is God's saving action happening today
and we want to express how much we depend on it;
we want to open ourselves to its power.

And so we pray …
deliver us
lest the evil in the world delude us;
keep us free
lest sin makes slaves of us;
protect us
lest anxiety eat into our trust in your providence.

Then Christ's good work may take effect in us,
in our faith and our conscience and our conviction.

As we wait in joyful hope for the coming of our Saviour

Waiting to hear from you
waiting at a bus stop
waiting for results
waiting for the rain to stop
waiting for the right moment
waiting for sleep to come …

But to 'wait in joyful hope
for the coming of our Saviour' –
a different kind of waiting,
and not just a far-off thing, rather
a waiting within all our waiting.

We know that he who came
will come again as he promised.
But we also know, because of this,
that the grace of his presence
can appear anywhere.

And so, whatever it is that we are waiting for,
we look for him in our waiting,
who gives all our waiting a quality of hope;
we wait in joyful hope.

In this spirit we pray –
may the eyes of our hearts be ever disposed
to see the signs of hope in our midst.

I leave you peace, my peace I give you
Let us offer each other a sign of peace

'I leave you peace.'
Nobody can say this but the Lord,
for this is God's peace
and there is nowhere else we could find it.

So, feel this peace being bestowed on you
falling on your head like a feather
into your hand like a flower
adding nothing of weight
yet taking a weight from you –
a gift.

And being invited to offer each other a sign of peace –
we do not so much give each other peace
(for peace is the Lord's to give);
rather our embrace is our happy recognition
of the peace we each are blessed with,
regardless of status,
in which we are one,
and which we can see in each other's faces.

Look not on our sins
but on the faith of your church

Sometimes you just have to look at a person
and realise that they are doing the best that they can.

God looks on us like that,
not on our sins, but on our desire,
our desire deep within
to be free, to be whole.

God looks on our struggling steps in that direction
and on our heart's slow opening
to let God's Spirit in.
God looks on our faith.

And when God does see our sin and smallness
God also sees a bigger picture –
the faith of others around us,
the faith in all the Body of Christ,
the cumulative beauty in all
and not just the isolated fall from grace.

So, when our own sinfulness leaves us dispirited,
may our hope be rekindled by the witness of others around us.

Lamb of God, you take away the sins of the world

'Like a lamb that is led to the slaughter' *(Isaiah 53:7)* –
he takes upon himself the weight of our sin.
We come to him with our heavy burdens
and he gives us rest –
we feel the burden of guilt being lifted,
we feel the lightness of being.

'The Passover lamb' –
as it was immolated
he was being crucified;
he is the lamb that is sacrificed
opening for us the door to freedom.

A lamb, so helpless, yet so strong –
'The Lamb at the centre of the throne
will be their shepherd
and he will guide them to springs
of the water of life
and God will wipe away
every tear from their eyes.' *(Revelation 7:17)*

Happy are those who are called to his supper

'Supper'
This is the heart of it, the Lord's Supper
(one of the first ever names for the Eucharist)
when we will do what he asked –
when we will 'take and eat' in memory of him.

'Happy'
We think of those Jesus called happy –
those who are poor; those who are poor in spirit;
those who mourn; those who weep at the lack of justice;
those who hunger and thirst for righteousness;
those who are merciful; those who are persecuted;
those who are pure in heart; those who are insulted.

'Those'
Those who are called;
it is not exclusive of anybody
and it is certainly not just 'us'.
We rejoice not just for ourselves
but with all who experience this invitation.

And we look around us – a community of such people,
open-hearted, waiting to be fed, wanting to be loved,
to be happy.

'Blessed are those who are called
to the marriage supper of the Lamb.' *(Revelation 19:9)*

Lord, I am not worthy to receive you,
but only say the word and I shall be healed

For some people 'I am not worthy'
is still a huge weight.
'I must go to confession first;
I must come to communion pure.'
In which case, why say this prayer?
Why not say, 'Lord, now that I am worthy …'?

From the start of Mass, and the words
'May almighty God have mercy on us',
we have been bathed in forgiving love.
All the Mass has been about allowing ourselves
to soak up this good news.

'I am not worthy' – in a sense, I will never be worthy.
The words come from the centurion
whose servant Jesus healed.
He could see what was what.
There is never a point at which I deserve God's love.
If I think I am at that point
I may be farther away than ever.

God's love is the gentle rain and I am the soil –
'as in a dry and weary land where there is no water' *(Psalm 63).*
God speaks the word that is like the rain;
and the healing happens.

I cannot be healed if I do not confess my wounds.
If I come confessing my health
will he not say, 'I have come to call
not the righteous but sinners'?

The Body of Christ

In times past people knelt, closed their eyes,
opened their mouth, put out their tongue,
received the host from the priest,
consumed it with dignity as they returned to their place,
knelt, closed their eyes,
put their head in their hands
and prayed in thanksgiving
for receiving the body of Christ.

Today people draw near, usually to a lay minister,
standing, with their eyes open and their mouth closed,
their hand outstretched to take the holy bread.
The minister may look into their eyes
as they say 'Body of Christ';
they might even smile,
they might even say your name.
And you might just smile in return
as you say Amen.

Returning to your place, you might look around
in wonder;
all these people, just like you, have just been told
who they are – body of Christ;
have just received this in their souls,
have just said Amen.

May almighty God bless you,
the Father, the Son and the Holy Spirit

According to Luke's gospel
Jesus' last act was to lift his hands and bless his disciples.
As he is carried up to heaven,
he leaves them full of joy,
blessing God in turn.

This is the spirit in which the Mass ends.

We began Mass by blessing ourselves
with the sign of the cross, the sign of the Trinity.
Now we present ourselves to be blessed
in the name of the Father, Son and Spirit.

We are blessed.
We are ready to go,
to return to the rest of our lives
full of joy
blessing God –
readied to live life differently,
ready to make a difference.

Go in peace

Like a stadium or concert hall emptying, we go;
nothing more to be had from staying around here.
'The Mass is ended.'

Except we don't just go;
we go in peace –
peace surpassing understanding,
a point of pure calm at the centre of our being,
the peace of Christ's salvation.

We don't just go in peace;
we are sent
'to love and serve the Lord' –
not to hoard what we have received
but to see to it that peace radiates outwards
by our living good lives.

Thanks be to God

We came together to give thanks
to 'eucharist'.
We have spoken the great prayer of thanks
at the heart of which
is Christ's own prayer of thanks
over bread and wine.

And now, as the priest says 'Go in peace'
we say 'Thanks be to God'
with an eye to *becoming* thanks,
to becoming Eucharist.

By living thankful lives,
by making thanks our first act in every situation,
in every prayer,
in every day,
in every mood,
by going about with grateful hearts
and a thankful outlook.

By all this,
we may have a transforming effect
on the mood around us
and the spirits of one another.

SECTION TWO

'Eucharist is ...'

This section is a series of meditations on the meaning of the Eucharist.
Each takes a different theme,
to explore the meaning from a different angle.
Each meditation concludes with a question for reflection.
This in turn may be experienced as an invitation into prayer.

Eucharist is … Joy

Already, before the Last Supper, we see the beginnings of Eucharist in the earthly life of Jesus. One of his most characteristic actions was his sharing of table with what the gospels call 'tax collectors and sinners'. These were people who were 'out in the cold' as a result of their way of living and of society's judgement on them. They had most likely lost all belief in themselves.

Jesus' gesture of sharing meals with them was simple but powerful. It said to them: 'you have a future'; 'you are a person'. It brought them in from the cold. They rediscovered their humanity. It was now impossible to be sad. The light came back into their lives. The joy returned to their faces. The love that was blocked up in their hearts was released. This transformation and overflowing is symbolised in the story of the sinner woman washing Jesus' feet (Luke, chapter seven).

The 'last' supper was the last in a long series of such occasions of joy. But the experience also continues in our Eucharist. Joy is at the heart of what we do. The priest says, 'Lift up your hearts!' We hear Jesus calling us in from the cold, to share table, to experience acceptance, to rediscover our humanity – to be happy!

'Happy are we who are called to his supper.' We thank the Lord for the Eucharist and for the joy it brings to our lives. May the Eucharist never cease to amaze us and transform us. May the welcome and warmth we experience from God make us happy and joyful. May that joy radiate from our hearts and our faces, to make the world a happier place.

For reflection
What it is like for Jesus to make you happy
when you encounter him in the Eucharist?

Eucharist is ... Being Sent

Have you ever thought about the meaning of the word 'Mass' – our more familiar word for Eucharist? It comes from the Latin word meaning 'sent'. This was used in the conclusion of the Latin Mass, '*Ite, missa est*' – 'Go, it is the dismissal'. The word 'mission' comes from here also. This alerts us to the intimate link between 'Mass' and 'mission', between participating in the Eucharist and 'being sent'.

When the priest says the final words of the Mass and sends us on our way, it is not just 'Go, the Mass is ended'. Rather, the Mass has now to be completed or fully accomplished by us. That is our mission. That is what we are sent forth to do. We are to bring the Eucharist with us – its joy, its grace, its harmony. This means that the Eucharist is not just 'for me'. It is also 'through me for you'. It is only when we bring the hope and love of the Mass into our relationships with others, that the Eucharist is fully celebrated.

Some parishes have a practice where Ministers of the Eucharist bring the Bread of Life from Sunday and weekday Masses to housebound people in the parish (many of whom have been joining in the celebration through parish radio). This practice is an invitation and challenge to all of us. We are all called to bring Eucharist with us, to nourish others just as we have been nourished ourselves. We are all sent.

The theme of being sent also links in with our Confirmation. Confirmation is about being sent. It is about baptised Christians assuming their share of the responsibility for the church's task of communicating the good news. We are invited to reflect on this mission which we all share. We are invited to think of ourselves as being sent. We are invited to feel ourselves being sent each time we celebrate the Eucharist together.

For reflection
What does it mean to you that we are called
'to bring Eucharist with us'?

Eucharist is ... Body of Christ

Sometime around the year 400, Saint Augustine gave a remarkable homily on the Eucharist. His audience was a group of newly baptised adults and he was telling them about the inner meaning of this mystery. He began with the question: 'How can this bread be Christ's body and what the chalice contains, his blood?'

He continued by quoting the words of Saint Paul, 'You are the body of Christ and his members.' He went on, 'If, therefore, you are the body of Christ and his members, *it is your own mystery that has been placed on the table of the Lord. It is your own mystery that you receive.*'

Then: 'To this which you are you respond "Amen" and, in responding, you accept it. What you hear is "the Body of Christ" and to this you respond "Amen". So, be a member of Christ's body, that your Amen may be true.' Later he says, '*Be what you see and accept what you are.*'

This is a great enrichment. When we hear 'body of Christ' we are used to thinking of the consecrated host, or of the physical body of Jesus when he walked the earth. We are less used to thinking of *ourselves*! And yet, this is what Paul and Augustine, two towering figures in our tradition, wanted to communicate to us – that we are Christ's body, that (in Augustine's words) '*It is the mystery of our peace and unity which he consecrates on his table.*'

When we return from receiving communion we pray quietly. Maybe there is something here to add to our meditation. Maybe we might think: 'Not only have I received communion – I have also entered into communion, as a member of the communion that is Christ's body.' Besides closing our eyes in prayer, we might also look up, at the body of Christ around us, and say, 'Amen.'

For reflection
Think about the meaning of the phrases from Augustine in italics.

Eucharist is ... Word of Life

In the past, a person could 'get' Mass if they arrived before the creed and left at Communion (without even receiving) – obligation fulfilled. In a sense, the Mass was the consecration. The word of scripture was secondary in our minds. Indeed, the Bible was seen as 'a Protestant book'. Catholics were not encouraged to read it.

In recent decades all has changed. We now speak of 'two tables' – the table of the Word of God and the table of the Body of Christ. We recognise that Christ is truly present in the word proclaimed. The word is more than words. It is a word that feeds and nourishes us. St John speaks of 'the word that is life' and of 'the word made flesh'.

Think of the power of words in our lives. 'You're wonderful!' 'How could you do that?' 'I'm delighted to see you.' 'Stop annoying me.' Words can build us up. They can bring us down. They can give us hope. They can be a lifeline. In the scriptures too, we hear a word, God's word. It is a word to give us hope, to comfort and challenge us, to warm our hearts, to lift our spirits, to inspire our thoughts and actions.

There is always something for us in the readings– even when we least expect it. A word, a phrase, an image, a story to connect with us where we are. When we learn to listen with our heart, the word will illuminate our lives. We can take it with us, and prolong our hearing of it, so that it speaks to us in the events of our lives. When that happens, the word is indeed made flesh and Christ is truly present.

When I hear your word, O Lord, may I feel its power; may I know its hope; may I rise to its challenge; may I radiate its joy.

For reflection
How could you develop your relationship with the Word of God?

Eucharist is... Initiation

Baptism, Confirmation and Eucharist are the three sacraments of 'initiation' for a Christian. In the early church it was an adult process and these three moments happened close to one another, and in that sequence. But for a long time now it has been a child-hood process, spread out over a dozen years or more, with First Communion preceding Confirmation.

Whatever the practice, initiation is not just once-for-all. It is an ongoing process. As long as life lasts, we are constantly being initiated further into the mystery, plumbing more and more deeply into the meaning of being a Christian. Eucharist is the 'hub' in our ongoing initiation.

John Paul II once spoke of the Eucharist as a mystery of light, a mystery of communion and a mystery of mission. Engaging with the Liturgy of the Word, we are gradually *enlightened* about what it means to be baptised. In the Liturgy of the Eucharist we grow in *communion* with Jesus and with one another as the Body of Christ. And each Mass ends with being sent, in a renewal of our confirmation *mission*.

How might we bring the awareness of initiation into our celebration? We could make more frequent use of the rites for sprinkling holy water and for renewing our baptism promises. But what might make the biggest difference is if Baptism and Confirmation and First Communion took place during Sunday Mass.

Every time that another person (child or adult) is baptised or confirmed or receives first communion, it holds up a mirror to the rest of us in the community. It is not just an event in their lives. It reflects back to us an ongoing process in all our lives. This could become an occasional and treasured part of our weekly gathering. In that case, Eucharist would be putting the larger community back in touch with its own journey of initi-ation.

For reflection
Can you see the Eucharist as developing your own
Baptism and Confirmation?

Eucharist is ... Hospitality

In George Herbert's famous poem, God is depicted as a host named 'Love'. Love is inviting me in to the feast, but I am resisting, feeling unworthy. Eventually Love's persuasion overcomes my feelings of shame. The poem ends, 'You must sit down, says Love, and taste my meat: so I did sit and eat.'

The poem conveys the hospitality of God that is the heart of the Eucharist. There is a place for each one of us at the Lord's table. God's welcome is unrestricted in its embrace. And what we taste when we accept the invitation is a foretaste of what will be our eternal delight at God's heavenly banquet.

Not everyone, though, feels the hospitality. There is a story about a man who came to Mass wearing a cap and did not take it off. One person suggested that he take it off, then another. But he did nothing. Outside the church the priest came over and asked him why he was wearing the cap at Mass. 'I've been coming to Mass here for over two years,' he said, 'and nobody has ever said as much as hello to me. But since I wore the cap, three people have spoken to me – that's progress!'

There are people who come to Mass who will only experience God's hospitality if they experience ours. The man in the story wanted to feel God's hospitality but could not. He needed to feel it in and through the welcome of those he was sitting beside. Are there others like him at Mass every weekend?

There are also people who do not come to Mass because they do not think that they are welcome. For one reason or another, they do not even approach the door – some circumstance in their life perhaps, or a feeling of being judged or unworthy. Many of them would love to know that the truth is otherwise, that they are more than welcome.

It is a wonderful discovery to experience the Eucharist as God's hospitality. It is to discover what God is like. It is also to discover what we ourselves are like – that we are wanted and welcome. And there is a third discovery – that there are others who depend on our welcome to feel God's hospitality.

For reflection
At Mass, do you feel yourself welcome and called to welcome?

Eucharist is ... Life-Giving

A friend tells this story about the birth of her first child. Her prevailing thought waiting in the hospital was, 'I don't mind what happens to me, as long as the baby is alright.' And indeed, everything went fine. It was near the weekend when the baby was born and on Sunday she felt well enough to go to Mass in the hospital oratory.

As she describes it, she felt herself filling up with a blaze of light when she heard the words of consecration, as if for the first time. 'This is my body given up for you ... this is my blood shed for you.' She exclaimed to herself, 'Jesus, I know what you mean!' Mass was never the same again.

Countless mothers have heard the words of consecration in the same way. In this they have glimpsed the profound connection between God's self-giving and ours. We are not meant to look on at the consecration like spectators at a show. We are meant to bring to it our own story of self-giving – the pain of letting go and giving ourselves to another; the joy of knowing that we have given new life to another person.

There is so much giving of self going on in our lives. It may not be as dramatic as a mother giving birth but it is no less amazing for that. Think of how children give so much life to others. Think of how generous friends can be in times of need. Think of how people who are suffering grace the lives of those around them.

If we bring to the Eucharist this awareness of our own self-giving, it helps us get in touch with what the consecration means. If we tune in to our own striving to live for others, we are able to appreciate more of the incredible self-giving of God. This moment of adoration becomes more precious when we bring to it a sense of wonder at who we are ourselves. Then we can pray to God: 'May Christ make us an everlasting gift to you.'

For reflection
Think of Jesus as life-giving for you,
and of yourself as life-giving for others.

Eucharist is ... Together

How many times do we say the word 'I' during Mass, compared to the word 'We'? We say, 'I confess to almighty God' and 'Lord I am not worthy', but there isn't a lot more after that. Whereas we are all the time saying 'we'.

In the Gloria, '*we* worship you ... *we* give you thanks ... *we* praise you for your glory'. In the Creed, '*we* believe in God ... *we* believe in one Lord Jesus Christ ... *we* believe in the Holy Spirit'. We say '*Our* Father ... give *us* this day *our* daily bread ...'. And we say, '*we* thank you for counting *us* worthy', as well as 'look not on *our* sins but on the faith of *your church*'. As Saint Cyprian put it, the Lord would not have us pray privately on our own; our prayer is public and for all, because we are all one.

The point is that the Eucharist is about 'we'. It is a communal event. The Word of God is not a private meditation, but a public proclamation that forms us as a community. 'Body of Christ', it is not just what we receive, it is what we become. 'Grant that *we*, who are nourished by his body and blood, may be filled with his Holy Spirit and become *one body*, one spirit in Christ.'

The original name, 'the breaking of bread', tells us that the Eucharist is an action we do together. It is a ritual at which we are all in a very real sense concelebrants. It can sometimes look like a collection of individuals engaged in separate private acts of public worship. Even when a person says gratefully that Mass is 'my quiet time' during the week, there is something missing. While the Eucharist is intensely personal, it is not private.

There is a challenge here. I cannot be satisfied with just going along and getting something out of it. If the Eucharist is a celebration together, then I need to reach out and engage with those around me. The Sign of Peace is one way of expressing this. I could also make sure to include the others around me in my prayer. I could make sure to smile at people and say hello. I could be somebody who is creating a feeling of community and welcome.

For reflection
How could we make our Eucharist more of a 'together' experience?

Eucharist is ... Breaking Bread

Just before Communion, the priest takes the host and breaks it. It is such a small action that most of us hardly notice it – and yet it is at the heart of the Eucharist. This phrase, 'the breaking of bread' is an expression that the very first Christians used to designate their Eucharistic assemblies.

In the Acts of the Apostles, Luke describes how they gathered for the breaking of bread. Just before this he tells the story of the Road to Emmaus, where two of the disciples encounter the risen Jesus, but only recognise him 'in the breaking of bread' – the very action Jesus had performed at the Last Supper.

'Breaking of bread' opens up a number of 'windows' into the rich meaning of the Eucharist. *'Bread broken is bread shared.'* A first meaning is that, in the breaking of bread, Jesus shares life with us. He shares *our* life with us – our feelings, hopes, disappointments. And he shares *his* life with us – feeding our hunger, sustaining our spirit.

Bread broken is bread shared. A second meaning is that we share bread with one another, the bread of life. We break bread and we become united – one bread, one body. This urges us to share life with one another also – to nourish each other's hunger and sustain each other's spirit.

Bread broken is bread shared. A third meaning is that bread broken refers to Jesus' body broken on the cross. When he breaks bread at the Last Supper, he says 'This is my body, given for you.' When we follow his command to 'do this in memory of me', we recognise him in the breaking of bread, he whose body was broken for us.

Bread broken is bread shared. A fourth meaning is that our breaking of bread reaches outwards, to feel the hunger of the world. Nourished by the Eucharist, we are invited to see ourselves as continuing Jesus' mission by bringing the bread of life to a hungry world.

For reflection
Which of these meanings of 'bread broken'
do you find most thought-provoking?

Eucharist is... Reconciliation

In the past we were very familiar with going to confession before going to Mass and communion. There was a feeling that we had to make ourselves worthy beforehand. The downside of this was that it lessened our sense of the Eucharist itself as a place of reconciliation.

But look at the words in our Eucharist and what they say:
'*Lord I am not worthy.*' We come here in order to *become* worthy.
'*May almighty God have mercy on us, forgive us our sins.*' Our prayer is that Mass will be a time of reconciliation.
'*Lamb of God, you take away the sins of the world.*' This 'taking away' is the very thing we celebrate at Mass.
'*This is the cup of my blood, shed so that sins may be forgiven.*' The words of consecration are words of forgiveness.
'*This sacrament which has made our peace with you.*' Eucharist is reconciliation.

The Eucharist is full of such language. 'Forgive us our trespasses.' 'Look not on our sins but on the faith of your church.' 'See the victim whose death has reconciled us to yourself.' It all adds up to saying that the Eucharist is the great event of reconciliation, the great sacrament of mercy and forgiveness.

We come to the Eucharist to be bathed in God's compassion. We come to be rid of our estrangement and isolation. We come to allow ourselves to be forgiven. 'Only say the word and I shall be healed.'

The Sign of Peace is part of all this. When we shake hands we enter into the 'communion' part of the Mass. We recognise the reconciliation that is happening. In communion we experience reconciliation – between each of us and God; among ourselves. 'In our peace, God's peace.'

The Eucharist is a powerful sacrament of reconciliation. So much so that we also have a separate sacrament totally dedicated to bringing home to us the good news of God's reconciling love!

For reflection
How have you experienced the Eucharist
as a sacrament of reconciliation?

Eucharist is ... Gathering

When the word 'church' was first used, back in New Testament times, it had few of the connotations it has today. It simply meant the Christians of a particular place who gathered for the Eucharist. The original word for church – *ekklesia* – means an assembly, people called together. The stress is on people gathering. As Christians, we are not just called; we are called together, gathered.

This is the background to efforts today to enhance the sense of 'gathering' around the beginning of the Mass. If being church means being gathered, then it is important how we gather. The way we gather is meant to reflect something of who we are. It should convey the joy and togetherness of being the body of Christ.

Instead of people coming unnoticed into the church, might there be a friendly face, distributing the leaflet perhaps? Instead of people just waiting for things to start, might we practise the music, to get us into the frame of mind? Instead of the priest slipping in a side door from the sanctuary, could we have a procession up the church, from among the gathered people, drawing us into a common focus? Perhaps, before the priest begins, might a layperson welcome us and present the theme of the day's worship?

Coming to Mass is about more than 'showing up'. It's about belonging, it's about togetherness, it's about hospitality. There is a human feel to it – human beings connecting with one another, aware that they are gathering together as Christ's body. If there is a human feel of 'gathering', then it is more likely that there will be a divine feel to it too – a feeling of God's hospitality, God's embrace, God's presence.

It's the same as any time we enter a room, or join a group, or come together for some occasion The way we do it matters. It says a lot about us. Gathering for the Eucharist is about feeling glad to be here, feeling good about being part of the Body. We don't just turn up; we gather!

For reflection
How important do you think it is to pay attention to how we gather?

Eucharist is ... Giving Thanks

When Jesus healed the ten lepers, only one returned to give thanks. Maybe that is the way life is. It's one thing to enjoy the gift, it's another to acknowledge the giver.

Giving thanks is a perspective on life, an attitude to life. It is about being able to stand back and appreciate the significance. As in the words from the film 'Babette's Feast': 'The moment comes when our eyes are opened, and we see that grace is infinite; grace demands nothing from us but that we shall await it with confidence and acknowledge it in gratitude.' A feeling of thanksgiving grows in the person who sees that life is grace.

The word 'Eucharist' means to give thanks. It comes from the Last Supper, where Jesus 'gave thanks' before giving the cup to his disciples. At the heart of what we are as human beings and as Christians is this act of thanksgiving, which we carry out in the spirit of Jesus.

So, what we do when we gather is done in a mood of deep appreciation. When we gather, it is in order to worship, to praise, to adore. Like the one leper, we have returned to the source of the gift, the cause of our wonder. In the words of the Gloria: 'We worship you, we give you thanks, we praise you for your glory.'

'Thanks' turns what we have into enough. It is the difference between 'having what you want' and 'wanting what you have'. To give thanks is to realise something of the magnitude of what we possess in Jesus Christ. With Saint Paul we say: 'Thanks be to God for his inexpressible gift.' *(2 Corinthians 9:15)*

If the Eucharist fills us with thanks, it leads us to go and live life thankfully, amidst all that life throws at us. Imagine what that would be like – to live life thankfully. Imagine the difference it would make to others if we lived life thankfully – just as Jesus' act of thanks makes a difference to us.

For reflection
How does the Eucharist help you to live life more thankfully?

53

Eucharist is ... Amazement

John Paul II said that 'a profound amazement' should always fill the community gathered to celebrate the Eucharist. It was his hope 'to rekindle this Eucharistic amazement'.

The Bible is a story of people being amazed again and again at God's power to bring new life out of darkness and desolation. In the Old Testament, as the people of Israel are exiled in Babylon, having lost everything, the prophet Isaiah has God proclaiming: 'I am about to do a new thing; now it springs forth; do you not perceive it?' *(Isaiah 43:19)* It is as if the deepest distress is the occasion for the most profound amazement.

When the disciples found the tomb empty, it was the first stirrings of amazement. 'Peter got up and ran to the tomb; stooping and looking in, he saw the linen cloths by themselves; then he went home, amazed at what had happened.' *(Luke 24:12)* This is the beginning of Christianity – an astonishment at the magnitude of what God has done in raising Jesus from the dead.

At the heart of being a believer is this feeling of being amazed. Again and again we have to escape from the temptation of routine religion, of taken-for-granted religion. Like sunbathing, we have to put ourselves in a place where the light can get at us! We have to allow ourselves to become amazed.

The Eucharist is the pinnacle of this. As John Paul put it, in the Eucharist there is 'a mysterious oneness in time' between the death and resurrection of Christ and ourselves two millennia later. We are doing more than remembering those events. We are in real contact with them, becoming amazed in the same way as Peter was. They are happening for us and amongst us.

When our Eucharistic amazement is rekindled, we will also experience a new amazement at all that God is doing in our lives and in our world. We will see God's creative power at work in the most surprising ways amidst human anguish and struggle. Hopefully that will lead to communicating to others something of the amazement that lies at the heart of who we are.

For reflection
What amazes you about the Eucharist?

Eucharist is … Real Presence

The first letter of John begins with the writer talking of 'what we have heard, what we have seen with our eyes, what we have looked at and touched with our hands – the word of life'.

The letter was written some seventy years after the death of Jesus. One has the impression of an old man vividly remembering something as tangible now as it was then. His words invite us to feel that the presence is as real for us as it was for him. Even though Jesus is 'absent', his presence is incredibly real.

Nevertheless, when we talk about the 'real presence' of Jesus in the Eucharist, there are many who experience an absence. Many cry, 'Where was God when…?' One cries, 'Where was God when I was inconsolable with grief?' Another, 'Where was God when others trampled on me?' Another, 'Where was God when the darkness was overpowering?' This suggests that we need to think about 'real presence' in a way that makes a link between Eucharist and life.

Our talk of 'real presence' revolves around the consecration. We say of the consecration that the sacrifice of the Cross is being made present. Yet the Cross too was an experience of absence, as Jesus cried, 'My God, my God, why have you forsaken me?' To proclaim in the Eucharist that Jesus is risen is to celebrate presence amidst absence and forsakenness.

So the real presence of the Eucharist is a celebration of the real presence of the Lord in our experience in the world. It is a presence that is often experienced as an absence. But it is real, because he has so completely identified with us in our agony and our troubles.

To say that Jesus is really present in the bread and wine is also to say that he is really present in the body, for 'one bread' means that we are one body, the body of Christ. 'Real presence' challenges us to be a real presence of hope for one another. What we hear, what we see with our eyes, what we touch with our hands, is one another. In that, his presence is real.

For reflection
What are the different ways in which Jesus is present in your life?

Eucharist is ... Communion

'Communion' has many meanings. It is, first of all, our communion with Jesus. But it is also communion among ourselves. When the minister says 'Body of Christ', we are being told what it is we are receiving. But we are also being told what we are and what we are to become. We are the Body of Christ, joined to one another in him.

This communion, however, is not confined to those who are physically present together. It is also a communion with those participating in other Masses in the parish. It is also a communion with those participating via radio, especially the sick or housebound.

We are also in communion with our sisters and brothers who are not participating in the Eucharist this weekend, or who participate only infrequently. Likewise, we are in communion with all those we pray for at Mass – in the prayers of the faithful, and in the intercessions of the Eucharistic Prayer.

Then there is our communion with those to whom we give. The special collections during the year – for the poor, for victims of disasters – are a powerful statement of compassion and solidarity.

We are also in communion with the wider diocesan family and with the church worldwide. This is symbolised in our prayers for the Pope and for our bishop. Our communion is not inward-looking or closed, but universal and inclusive.

Very special is our communion with those who have died. They figure prominently in our prayers at Mass, prayers which bring to mind the 'Communion of Saints'. This puts us in touch with the origin and destiny of all our communion – the communion of love that is Father, Son and Spirit.

Sometimes the church is called the 'Mystical Body of Christ'. Previously, it was the Eucharist that was the mystical body (and the church the 'true body'). Partly because there are so many meanings to its communion beyond what we might appreciate at first sight.

For reflection
What 'communion' do you feel when you participate in the Eucharist?

Eucharist is ... Enough

In the story of the loaves and fishes, Andrew says to Jesus, 'There is a boy here who has five barley loaves and two fishes. But what are they among so many people?' The disciples are saying, 'But all we have is ...' Then they discover that there is enough. This is a story about the Eucharist.

It tells us that our offering – whatever it is, however paltry – is enough. At the presentation of gifts, we bring everything that we are. If we have little to celebrate in our lives, we bring that little. And if we have nothing, we bring that nothing. Because in God's hands, all is made good. In God's hands, what we bring becomes enough.

A transformation happens – in the story and in the Eucharist. The transformation is this: what we offer becomes what he gives. 'Give and it will be given to you. A good measure, pressed down, shaken together, running over, will be put into your lap; for the measure you give will be the measure you get back.' *(Luke 6:38)*

'Enough' also has wider connotations, when we think of the meaning of 'enough' in our world. There are some people who can never get enough. There are millions upon millions who don't have enough. And the world as a whole has more than enough for everybody.

There is a disturbing alliance of abundance and hunger in our world. There is enough and there isn't enough. We are led to think of the Eucharist as bread for a hungry world. We think of ourselves becoming bread, becoming as nourishing as bread for one another and for the world.

For this to happen, we have to believe in ourselves. I have to believe that who I am is enough. This too is miracle; what we are is enough – because, by his presence, what we are is transformed into life-giving bread for others.

For reflection
What link do you see between the feeding in the Eucharist
and the hunger in the world?

Eucharist is ... Transformation

At the presentation of the gifts during the Mass, what do we bring to the altar? Bread and wine, certainly, but what else? Think of the hymn, 'In bread we bring you, Lord, our bodies' labour; in wine we offer you our spirit's grief ...' Are we not also bringing and offering ourselves? As in that other hymn, 'All that I am ... I offer now to you'.

If that is true, then it affects our idea of what it is that is 'changed' with the consecration. The bread and wine become the body and blood of Christ. But what do we become, we who have also been placed on the altar? We too, as Saint Paul tells us, are changed into the Body of Christ.

So, a very important part of the change is that we are transformed. We are not onlookers, watching something happen. We are involved, we are part of the drama, we are part of the transformation. By our participation, we undergo a change ourselves, into the mystery of what we most deeply are. In the spirit of Ignatius of Antioch: 'I am his wheat, ground fine, to be made purest bread for Christ.'

This implies a connection with the way we live our lives. A Christian way of life is characterised by change and transformation. John Paul II said that 'What is needed is a continuous, permanent conversion.' Cardinal Newman said that to live is to change and to be perfect is to have changed often. Being a Christian means allowing myself to undergo a lifelong process of being changed into what I am meant to be.

In the Eucharist, our daily programme of change is revealed in its full significance. It is something that reaches into another sphere of being, a process of being transformed into Christ.

For reflection
What does it mean to say that we, as well as bread and wine,
are changed?

Eucharist is ... Rest

Eucharist is part of our Sunday 'rest'. Some people talk of it as their special 'quiet time' in the week. It is good to realise that rest of this kind is a higher kind of activity than working. It is a heightened state of being and of consciousness.

Part of the idea of the Sabbath rest was to stand back from the relationships of oppression that build up almost inevitably in our interpersonal bonds and in our society. In the Eucharist, the penitential rite has this spirit – a space where we can confess how relationships have become oppressive. In that space we can connect again with God's liberating grace.

If we rest and stand back, it also allows us to see how things may have got out of focus in our lives. We can be so busy, whether about important or unimportant things. In the process we become scattered in ourselves, scattered in different directions, with a diminished sense of a centre to it all.

This is where the Liturgy of the Word helps us to 'gather' ourselves again. Listening to the scripture re-centres us on the heart of our calling. The homily invites us to discern what message the Word has for us. If we listen with an open heart, God's Spirit will help focus our energies on what really matters.

Standing back in a restful way also enables us to see the grace in life again. The Eucharistic Prayer, because it is a prayer of thanksgiving, opens our eyes to the grace. We 'lift up our hearts' to look beyond the struggles, the monotony, the disappointments, to see the grace that is ever-present, steadfast and reliable, ever capable of surprising us.

Learning to rest in this way will change our lives. We live in a world of restlessness, where everything becomes work, even rest itself. If Eucharist is a time of rest, heightening awareness and centring us again, we can learn to be at rest even when we are working.

For reflection
How does Eucharist help to make all my living restful?

Eucharist is ... Sharing the Cup

In the gospel we hear Jesus saying, 'Those who eat my flesh and drink my blood abide in me.' At the Last Supper, after the bread, he takes the cup of wine and says, 'This is my blood of the covenant.' Is the emphasis in our Eucharist as it should be? We focus largely on the bread, the body. The wine, the blood, seem secondary – particularly in the communion rite of the Mass.

It is worth exploring, therefore, how the wine/blood theme expresses what is happening. Blood may not be an attractive topic, yet it is strongly symbolic of self-giving and self-sacrifice. One has only to think of a mother giving birth. There are also ancient echoes of how blood is symbolic of a bond made, a covenant sealed.

Then there is the theme of wine. Wine is about 'conviviality' – a word that literally has to do with living as one. It takes us back to Jesus' own image of he being the vine and we the branches. As Saint Augustine puts it: 'Many grapes hang from the vine, but all the juice flows into one. And that is what Jesus Christ means to us. He wants us to belong in him, to pour into him as one.'

Another aspect is opened to us by Jesus' question to his disciples: 'Are you able to drink the cup that I am about to drink?' To partake of the cup is to take up the cross. It symbolises following his path and imitating his way and becoming one with him. It means sacrifice, dying to self so that community may be born.

All of this suggests that communion with both bread and cup should be the normal practice. It helps us realise that Mass is about doing something together –namely, breaking bread and sharing the cup. To do both, rather than one only, is so obviously natural, and helps us engage at a deeper level with the meaning of the moment.

For reflection
What does receiving from the chalice add
to your experience of Eucharist?

Eucharist is ... Remembering

Jesus said, 'Do this in memory of me'. Our Eucharist is an act of remembering. In the scripture we remember the things he said, the meals he shared, his many interactions with people, the effect he had. If we listen with the heart, all these events come to life again. We are in the stories. They are happening for us.

In the Eucharistic Prayer we remember the outcome of his life. 'Father, calling to mind the death your Son endured for our salvation, his glorious resurrection and ascension into heaven ...' In calling to mind, we 'see the Victim whose death has reconciled us'. The one who died and is risen, is now in our midst.

This is a special kind of remembering, far more than a 'memorial service' or 'fond memories from the past'. It is a kind of remembering that makes the past present. 'Christ has died; Christ is risen.' In the same spirit as the Passover, what is remembered is a present reality. *Today* he is conquering death and sin; *today* the risen Lord interacts with us.

It is also a remembering that makes the future present – 'Christ will come again.' His resurrection is a kind of 'first fruits' and we look forward to the day when 'all things will be subjected to him', when 'God will be all in all' *(1 Corinthians 15:20-28)*. To remember the past is to remember our future. It is to remember our hope, and the hope he holds for the world and its ultimate transformation.

In making the past present and in making the future present, remembering makes the present different. Looking back intensifies our faith. Looking forward ignites our hope. With faith and hope fired up, we can look around us with a new energy of love. With memory transformed by hope, we are filled with the Spirit, geared up to play our part in making the dream come true.

For reflection
What do you think Jesus was hoping for when he said
'Do this in memory of me'?

Eucharist is ... Flesh and Blood

God communicates with us in a way that we can relate to. In the words of Saint John, 'The Word became flesh and lived among us.' God takes on a shape that we can recognise and be at home with, flesh and blood. That is 'incarnation'. What is sacred is communicated to us through what is most familiar to us.

We are, after all, physical beings, flesh and blood. We are bodily and we operate through our bodies – through what's tangible, visible, palpable, audible. With the incarnation, God has made this our gateway opening out into mystery. Our flesh-and-blood reality is filled with spirit.

Eucharist is the 'today' of incarnation. Jesus says, 'This is my body, for you' – the amazing in the ordinary, the godly in the worldly. What happened two thousand years ago is happening now. We find the sacred in what is most familiar – bread and wine. That which is most familiar is blessed, holy, consecrated.

Living the Eucharist is about rejoicing in this. If the word is made flesh, then all that is flesh, all that is bodily and worldly, is steeped in mystery. Eucharist celebrates the incarnation that is always 'now' and invites us to live in that spirit.

When we touch and feel; when we taste or smell; when we see or hear; we do so with a new awareness and insight. The earth we walk on, we tread with a new gentleness. The world we live in, we inhabit with a new attentiveness to its well-being. The other whom we encounter, we greet with a new sense of mystery. We reverence the sacred in what is most familiar, just as we reverence God in bread and wine, for God is given to us in flesh and blood.

For reflection
How does Eucharist help you to find 'the amazing in the ordinary'?

Eucharist is ... Service

Jesus performed two symbolic actions at the Last Supper – he broke bread and he washed the disciples' feet. When we think about the origin and meaning of the Eucharist, we link it more immediately to the breaking of bread. We are more inclined to see the washing of feet as applying to our call to serve one another in daily life.

The following words of John Paul II, however, may give us pause for thought: *'By bending down to wash the feet of his disciples, Jesus explains the meaning of the Eucharist unequivocally.'* It is John's gospel that recounts the washing of feet – and only John's gospel. It does so instead of recounting the breaking of bread, which we are told about in the other three gospels.

This is John's way of bringing out the profound meaning of the Last Supper. The washing of feet highlights that the Eucharist itself is an act of service. It is service on God's part, God washing our feet. This is another way for us to think about what the consecration means. It is Jesus saying, 'I am here for you; I put my life at your service.'

When we go to communion, we are making our response. We are allowing God to wash our feet. We are saying 'yes' to God's great act of ministry. We are agreeing to letting ourselves be ministered to.

In so doing, we define who we are. Our deepest identity lies in being ministered to by God and then ministering to one another in turn. We assent to Jesus' vision, that life is about serving and being served, about the giving and receiving of ministry. Eucharist is service; life is service.

For reflection
What link do you see between Jesus' two actions at the Last Supper?

Eucharist is ... Song of the People

Sometimes the Eucharist is called the 'Sunday Liturgy'. 'Liturgy' comes from a Greek word that means 'the work of the people'. Of course, what God is doing is at the heart of the Eucharist. But this idea of 'the work of the people' suggests a level of activity and participation on our part that might surprise us.

The word 'liturgy' says to us that the Eucharist is something we are *doing* rather than something we are only attending or watching (or watching somebody else doing). It also tells us that Eucharist is something we are doing *together* rather than something we are engaged in individually or privately. What we are doing together can be described in different ways – 'breaking bread'; 'giving thanks'; 'remembering'; 'celebrating'.

In that doing together, in our shared action, the mystery is encountered. Perhaps more than anything else, singing stands for this. Singing together is the most dramatic expression of our sense of 'liturgy', of celebrating together. Liturgy, the work of the people, is the song of the people.

There is an ancient saying, that 'the one who sings well prays twice'. We might add, that when we sing well *together* we pray thrice! Singing together connects us in a deeper way – to the mystery and to one another. As Saint Augustine put it, we are a new people and so we sing a new song. We sing with our mouths, with our hearts, with our lives. We are a living song of praise to the One who has taken us out of darkness into the Light.

How can we grow into this mindset? When it comes to singing in church, the official 'policy' today is that primacy should go to singing the parts of the Mass together – such as the psalm, the 'Holy Holy', the proclamation of faith, the great Amen. Listening to a choir is delightful, but secondary. It is more important that we sing than that we listen. Mass is not being done 'for us' by others. It is the song of the people.

For reflection
What difference does it make when we all join in the singing?

Eucharist is ... Priestly Action

When the New Testament talks about Christian priesthood, it makes two references. The first is to Christ as the one high priest 'who has offered for all time a single sacrifice' (*Hebrews 10:12*). The other is to Christians in general as a 'holy priesthood to offer spiritual sacrifices acceptable to God through Jesus Christ' (*1 Peter 2:5*).

The 'priesthood' as we know it came later. The special role and dignity of the priest at Mass lies in representing both of these New Testament priesthoods, that of Christ and that of Christ's followers. He speaks and acts in the person of Christ – so that it is Christ who speaks to us through him. And he speaks and acts on behalf of all Christ's priestly people – so that it is we who speak to God through him.

We see the priest as both representing Christ and his giving to us, and as representing us and our giving to Christ. On the one hand, he concentrates us on the priesthood of Christ, through which God's love is poured into our hearts. On the other, he concentrates us on our own priesthood, whereby our love rises like incense to God. In that way the Eucharist becomes a merging of our priestly sacrifice into that of Christ.

The *Catechism* throws light on the difference between the priesthood of the ordained minister and that of all Christ's followers. The latter exercise their priesthood by living their baptism, with lives of faith, hope and love, in the power of the Spirit. What is different about the ministerial priesthood is that it is at the service of the priesthood of all, encouraging, animating, activating it.

So the Eucharist is a priestly action in more ways than one. It is the 'today' of Christ's priestly and life-giving gift of his life. It is our offering of ourselves as 'a living sacrifice to God' (*Romans 12:1*). And it is the action of the priest as the focal point at which all priesthood becomes one single act of worship and praise.

For reflection
What does it mean to say that we are all priests at Mass?

Eucharist is ... A Meal

The meal is a favoured image for the Eucharist today, though it can be difficult to feel that in a big church congregation on a Sunday. Yet it captures very well the experience of the very first Christians, when they gathered in their own houses, in small numbers, and brought their own bread for the ritual. At a very early stage, the occasion included both a meal and a ritual around bread and wine.

Another difficulty with the meal image today is that a lot of our own eating is functional and non-social, hardly deserving the description 'meal'. Likewise, of course, there is a lot of functional, non-social 'getting Mass' on the part of Christians! But the meals we need to think of are our special meals – the special occasions that we mark with a meal. They are times for celebrating who we are, for confirming our love, for bonding together.

Many such occasions are family events and, on a larger scale, the parish is a family – the particular family of Christ's followers that gather in this place for Eucharist. If we can see the worshipping assembly as a family, it helps us see ourselves in a social way, gathering for a special occasion – to celebrate who we are, to confirm our faith and our love, to be bonded as one, in one hope.

Ultimately, the image comes from Jesus – from the Last Supper and from the many meals he was so fond of sharing with people. Exclusive is what they were not, neither in the sense of being confined to an elite, nor in the sense of certain people not being welcome. What they were was refreshing and hopeful, for whoever was open-hearted enough to take up what was being offered.

Eucharist is a meal in that spirit, actualising the same hope. But there is another dimension. Jesus also *spoke* about meals, in the way he imaged the 'banquet' of God's heavenly kingdom. Maybe, then, Eucharist is and is not a meal. Maybe it is a foretaste – like the smell of a special dinner, all the aroma but also shot through with expectation of what is not yet!

For reflection
What do you like about 'meal' as an image for the Eucharist?

Eucharist is ... Offering

In the early centuries there were quite a few names for the Eucharist, one of which was 'Offering'. While the word 'Mass' came to be the normal term, 'Offering' prevailed in the Celtic Church, as can be seen in the similar-sounding Irish word for the Mass – *Aifreann*. Just as 'Mass' focuses on the theme of sending, and 'Eucharist' on that of thanksgiving, so *Aifreann* directs our attention to the theme of offering.

'Offer' is a gracious word. We offer help, we offer sympathy, we offer a suggestion. It suggests a gentle reaching out; generously giving, yet respectfully restrained. The word reflects the spirit of how we are meant to be with one another. In the Mass it reflects how we are with God, and how God is with us.

It begins with the prayer, 'Through your goodness we have this bread/wine to offer.' Then we ask God 'to accept this offering'. We call on the Holy Spirit to 'sanctify these offerings'. And after the consecration the priest says: 'We offer you this life-giving bread, this saving cup'; 'We offer you in thanksgiving this holy and living sacrifice.'

What is offered is Christ's own offering – 'We offer you his body and blood, the acceptable sacrifice which brings salvation to the whole world.' To his offering we join ourselves – and so the priest can also say, 'May he make us an everlasting gift to you.' We ourselves are caught up in the mystery of offering, the mystery of *An t-Aifreann*.

There is a religious congregation called the Oblates – a word coming from the same Latin root as *Aifreann*, and meaning to offer or to present. They remind us of our calling to find ourselves in giving ourselves. We might think also of the poor widow Jesus speaks of, putting her two copper coins into the treasury. It is not the material size of the offering, but the spiritual quality, in the spirit of God's own graciousness, that makes it *Aifreann*.

For reflection
Who offers what in the Eucharist?

Eucharist is ... Source and Summit

The Vatican Council described the Eucharist as the summit towards which all the life of the Christian community is directed, and as the source from which all its life flows. The imagery is suggestive of a mountain peak and of the source of a river (which itself is often high up a mountain).

As 'summit', the Eucharist is our focal point. It is the defining moment, expressing everything that we are, holding the object of all our hopes and struggles, and anticipating their future transformation. As 'source', it is where we do not rest, where we set out again, enlightened and motivated for the journey.

In a similar vein, the Eucharist is both 'end' and 'means'. As an end it is like the summit. Nothing beyond it, it is a moment of pure thanks and praise. But it is not an end in itself as if nothing else were important. It is also a means to an end. It is meant to bear fruit in Christian living to make the world a better place, more likened to God's kingdom.

Another angle sees the Eucharist as both 'background' and 'foreground'. It belongs in the background in that what really matters is Christian living in the world. In this sense, our life as a worshipping community plays a supporting role to our life as a ministering and missionary community.

But the Eucharist also belongs in the foreground, in that it is where past and future meet. It is the meeting point of our own source in the death and resurrection of Christ and our own summit in the heavenly banquet. It is the 'still point of the turning world', our glimpse of ultimate transformation.

We try to hold these in balance or creative tension – source and summit, end and means, background and foreground. In the story of the Transfiguration, Peter says, 'It is good for us to be here' – he wants to stay. But we cannot stay, we must return to the details of ordinary life. That is where we belong, until the time comes, beyond our imagining or calculating, when we will remain and venture forth no more.

For reflection
How do you experience this 'creative tension' in your life?

Eucharist is ... Participation

Saint Paul says that the bread that we break and the cup that we bless are a sharing in the body and blood of Christ (*1 Corinthians 10:16*). 'Sharing' translates a Greek word *koinonia* meaning a communion or a sharing or a participation. We are not just 'receiving communion'. We are entering into a communion, participating in the mystery of being at a very deep level.

If I am 'participating in the Body of Christ', this suggests a very full engagement of my self. Eucharist is about being taken up into this sphere and mode of existence – namely, into the 'Body of Christ'. There, I find that I am most fully myself by being brought beyond myself. Eucharist is about 'breakthrough' into this sphere and finding that ours is more than a merely human existence.

From the early centuries Christians spoke about 'divinisation'. The word says that becoming a Christian is about entering into our divinity. It sees that the meeting of human and divine, which happens uniquely in Christ, does not happen only in Christ, but is meant for all. The purpose of the incarnation is so that God may be born in each of us, and that each of us be born into God.

This throws light on what the Vatican Council announced as the goal of 'full, conscious and active participation' of all in the Eucharist. Such participation goes beyond spectator-like passivity. But that does not mean just doing things at Mass, like the various ministries within the celebration. You do not have to be 'doing' something in order to participate.

The one who is participating most intensely may outwardly appear to be doing nothing at all! Participation is about your quality of being present. You have a sense of what is happening and of what you are engaging in. You are alive to the mystery you are participating in. You know in some embryonic way that you are part of the mystery.

For reflection
How has the quality of your participation in the Eucharist changed over the years?

Eucharist is ... Embrace

One of the most lavish meals in the gospels begins with a huge embrace. 'While he was still far off, his father saw him and was filled with compassion; he ran and put his arms around him and kissed him.' *(Luke 15:20)* Something so ecstatic about somebody being welcomed in from the cold.

In our Eucharist, the nearest we get to an embrace is at the sign of peace when we shake hands, or occasionally hug one another. It comes quite late in the service, so it does not have a great effect on the mood of the occasion. Even in those Catholic rites where it comes at the presentation of the gifts, things are already well under way.

Yet, the Eucharist is an embrace! When Jesus says, 'It will be shed for you and for all', he is being so inclusive. You can never be so far out in the cold that you are no longer within the reach of this embrace. Embrace encapsulates the whole story and spirit of the Bible, of salvation; God reaching out to hold us to God's heart. 'Come to me all you that are weary and are carrying heavy burdens.' *(Matthew 11:28)*

Embrace signals peace. 'For he is our peace. He came and proclaimed peace to you who were far off and peace to those who were near.' *(Ephesians 2:14,17)* It puts us in touch with our oneness, with God and with one another, deeper than our differences, our hurts and our suspicions.

Perhaps there should be a sacred moment, much earlier than the sign of peace, when we embrace, when there is a spotlight on inclusivity, when all can be 'felt into peace'. Some know it and do not need it. Some have it and do not know it. Some need it and do not know it.

For reflection
When have you been at Mass and felt yourself being embraced?

Eucharist is ... Food for the Journey

There is a rite called 'viaticum' which is a celebration of the Eucharist to mark the dying person's passage into eternal life. It means 'food for the journey'. As one of its prayers says: 'When the hour comes for us to pass from this life, Jesus strengthens us with this food for the journey and comforts us by this pledge of his resurrection.'

In a sense, every Eucharist is 'viaticum', food for the journey. The Bible tells us about Elijah, struggling, unable to go on. An angel touches him and tells him to eat, 'or the journey will be too much for you'. He finds beside him a cake baked on hot stones and a jar of water – 'then he went in the strength of that food forty days and forty nights to Horeb the mountain of God' (1 Kings 19).

This is food, not just to get us to our destination, but also to help us on the journey itself. The story of the manna in the desert says as much. Every person was to gather so much each day, but some were greedy and others lost out. Yet, when they measured it, 'Those who gathered much had nothing over and those who gathered little had no shortage.' (Exodus 16) Food for the journey is more than a private affair.

In other words, what we receive we share, and what we share is food for our journey together. When we break bread together in the Eucharist, we are bonded together and strengthened to live life in solidarity as members of Christ's Body. This food nourishes us, not just in giving us individual energy, but in giving us an orientation towards one another.

At every Mass we say, 'give us this day our daily bread'. In receiving our daily bread we are made into one body. We are, literally, 'companions' – a word formed from the Latin words for 'bread' and 'with'. Breaking bread together, we are companions on the journey. And in the quality of our companionship we already experience something of the joy of reaching our destination.

For reflection
In what way does the Eucharist support you for the journey?

Eucharist is ... Celebration

The phrase 'celebrating' the Eucharist could have either of two meanings. The weaker meaning of 'celebrate' is to perform or officiate at a ceremony. The stronger meaning is to mark an occasion – a happy occasion, a special occasion – with festivities.

We might also remember the language we formerly used – 'saying' Mass, 'hearing' Mass, 'going to' Mass, 'getting' Mass, 'attending' Mass, being 'at' Mass. When we spoke like that, a ceremony was being performed, somebody was officiating. Clearly, it was a celebration in the weaker sense above.

Was it also a celebration in the stronger sense? Part of what is changing is that we are trying to bring out that stronger sense – of a special and happy occasion, with a palpable sense of rejoicing and gladness and festivity.

It is a moot point to what extent those present experience themselves as celebrating in this stronger sense. There are those for whom it is an observance, even a penance, more duty than pleasure, more routine than special. Even among those who do feel it to be 'special', their sense of it can be anywhere on a spectrum from joy-filled to gloomy.

But it sounds odd to talk about the Eucharist as a celebration in the strong sense. We associate celebration with big occasions like anniversaries and victories and transitions – after which we revert to 'normal mode'. They are highpoints, occasional, not that frequent. Yet we celebrate the Eucharist every week; for some people it is daily. How can celebration be so often?

It is because celebration is meant to be a constant mood for Christians. Faith is not just believing in something; it is rejoicing in something, rejoicing that Christ is risen from the dead, rejoicing in all that means for us. Everyday Christian living is shot through with a mood of thanksgiving, a feeling of being blessed.

It isn't a case of 'that was the celebration; now we get on with living'. Rather, the celebration returns us to the source of our constant mood. We take time to delight in the One who has given us such cause for rejoicing, such reason to be happy.

For reflection
What do you have to celebrate at the Eucharist?

Eucharist is ... Amen

Is there anything in the Mass that we say as often as 'Amen'? We say it about a dozen times, so it deserves consideration. In our usage it means 'so be it', but it is more than a lifeless or submissive assent. It has a strong sense of commitment, of desiring that the preceding prayer be heard. It is a 'Yes' spoken with all our heart.

'Amen' is our yes to what the Eucharist means, our yes to Christ's coming among us, our yes to peace and healing, our yes to Christ taking us by the hand to follow his way. Eucharist is an act of 'Yes', in the spirit of Mary at the Annunciation: 'Let it be with me according to your word.'

But our yes is caught up in a greater yes, God's own 'Yes' to us in Christ. 'For the Son of God, Jesus Christ, was not "Yes and No"; but in him it is always "Yes". For in him every one of God's promises is a "Yes". For this reason it is through him that we say the "Amen", to the glory of God.' *(2 Corinthians 1:19-20)*

The original Hebrew word means true, faithful, certain. It implies sureness, firmness. And when Jesus sometimes prefaces what he says with 'Amen', it is because he himself is the Amen of God to us, the assurance of what we believe and hope for.

Jesus is also humanity's Amen to God, revealing to us what we also can be. In the prayer 'Through him, with him, in him', which concludes with the Great Amen, we are joining ourselves to the 'Yes' to God that was Jesus' life and death. Our own Amen to God rests on this sure foundation.

Amen is also the last word in the Bible. Will it be the last word ever? Was it Jesus' last word on the cross? Will it be our last word? It begins now, in our 'Amen' at the Eucharist. It flows into our living as Christ's Body, so that our Amen may be true.

For reflection
What power and energy do you feel in the word 'Amen'?

Eucharist is … Work of the Spirit

The Holy Spirit has been called 'the go-between God'. Already at work in the creation of the world. Linking divinity and humanity in the incarnation. 'By the power of the Holy Spirit he took flesh and was born of the Virgin Mary.' Poured out into the world through Christ's resurrection. The Spirit forms the link between us and the risen Lord, making his resurrection a present experience.

It is this Spirit that we call upon in the Eucharist. 'We bring you these gifts. We ask you to make them holy by the power of your Spirit, that they may become the body and blood of your Son.' The go-between God crafts our encounter with Jesus. Through the Spirit, the risen Jesus is a present reality. Through the Spirit we experience what the disciples experienced on the road to Emmaus.

Having called on the Spirit in this way, we go on to ask more. 'Grant that we, who are nourished by his body and blood, may be filled with his Holy Spirit, and become one body, one spirit in Christ.' The go-between God goes on to craft communion, drawing us into the mystery. 'By your Holy Spirit gather all who share this one bread and one cup into the one body of Christ, a living sacrifice of praise.'

The mystery we are drawn into is the Trinity. If the Spirit puts us in communion with the risen Jesus, then we are brought into communion with the life of the Trinity. Through the power of the go-between God, we find Jesus' promise to us coming true: 'Those who love me will keep my word, and my Father will love them, and we will come to them and make our home with them.' *(John 14:23)*

Father, Son and Spirit dwell in our hearts. We in turn dwell in God, born into the life of the Trinity. As somebody put it, each of us becomes a 'fourth face' of God. This is the amazing truth of the Eucharist and it is also our calling: to allow the Spirit make each of us into an epiphany or manifestation of divine loving.

For reflection
How would you describe the role of the Holy Spirit in the Eucharist?

Eucharist is ... Blessing

Grace before meals: 'Bless us O Lord and these thy gifts, which of thy bounty we are about to receive, through Christ our Lord Amen.' Or, as the children learn today: 'Bless us O God as we sit together. Bless the food we eat today. Bless the hands that made the food. Bless us O God. Amen.' The prayer has a feel of blessing and being blessed, of gift and appreciation.

It also reflects the spirit of prayer in the culture Jesus grew up in. Prayer had that same feel of blessing, and blessing was at the heart of prayer. The family meal was a principal moment for prayer and blessing. This is the backdrop to Jesus' last supper meal with his 'family' of disciples.

Mark tells us that 'he took a loaf of bread and after blessing it he broke it, gave it to them and said, 'Take: this is my body.' At the supper in Emmaus, Luke tells us that the risen Lord 'took bread, blessed and broke it, and gave it to them'; and in this they recognised him. The blessing prayer has a new focus, on the gift of God in Jesus. It becomes 'Eucharist', a new prayer of thanks.

Blessing is at the heart of Eucharist, which originally was a prayer of thanks over the gifts. First, we bless God: 'Blessed are you, Lord God of all creation, through your goodness we have this bread to offer.' Then we ask God to bless our offering; 'Bless and approve our offering ... you give us all these gifts, you fill them with life and goodness, you bless them and make them holy.'

We conclude the Mass by asking God to bless us, to 'let us be filled with every grace and blessing'. We go with a blessing. We go blessing Jesus. We go to be a blessing. 'Blessed is he who comes in the name of the Lord.' Blessed are we who go in his name.

For reflection
What do the words 'bless'/'blessing' mean to you?

Eucharist is … Healing

In one interpretation of the well-known story, Jesus himself is the good Samaritan and we are the ones he lifts up from the side of the road and carries to the inn; it is our wounds that he heals. The story happens today, when we see the Eucharist as our inn, our place of hospitality, where Jesus brings us to be healed.

Early in the Mass the priest says, 'You were sent to heal the contrite.' Later on we ask, 'Only say the word and I shall be healed.' There is a prayer for before Communion, by Thomas Aquinas, in this spirit:

As one who is infirm, I draw near to the healer of life
As one who is unclean, to the fountain of mercy
As one who is blind, to the light of eternal brightness
As one who is poor and needy, to the Lord of heaven and earth.

We ask him to heal, not only ourselves and our relationship to God, but also our relationships with one another. 'Hear the prayers of the family you have gathered here before you; in mercy and love unite all your children wherever they may be.' The Sign of Peace can be seen as a recognition of our call to be a community of healing.

'Healing' and 'saving' are intimately linked, as is reflected in the Irish word *slánú*. They are about the total, fully-rounded well-being that God passionately desires for us – social, spiritual, physical, emotional, mental. They are about wholeness and happiness, for each individually and for all of us together.

Jesus is 'the wounded healer' who has brought about our *slánú*. In the Eucharist he calls on us to be wounded healers in a different sense. He calls on us to experience our own healing in a way that puts us in touch with the wounds of other and with the well of divine compassion within ourselves.

For reflection
How have you experienced the Eucharist as a sacrament of healing?

Eucharist is ... Heavenly

Occasionally, prayers in the Mass are directed to the afterlife, for instance: 'Lord ... bring us to the eternal life we celebrate in this Eucharist.' This may not resonate with many people today. Our concerns tend to be for this life. At the same time, we could lose sight of the longer horizon.

When, after their years in the desert, the people of Israel crossed over the Jordan, 'they ate the produce of the land ... the manna ceased on that day' *(Joshua 5:11-12)*. Likewise for us, the Eucharist is our transitional food; it is for now, it is not our permanent condition. What we have now is more like a 'home from home'. In celebrating Eucharist we also long for our greatest hope to be satisfied. We say: 'When we eat this bread and drink this cup, we proclaim your death Lord Jesus, until you come again.'

St Gregory the Great likened Christian existence to a dawn state, between the night of unbelief and the splendour of heavenly brightness. 'Dawn announces that night has already passed, but it does not display the full brightness of day; while it is dispelling the one it is welcoming the other, and it keeps light and darkness intermingled.'

Eucharist is like experiencing the dawn – a pristine moment of unspoiled beauty, but still a harbinger of the day, when it itself will be no more. We celebrate Christ's death and resurrection, the victory of the light over the darkness of sin and death. The victory is won, but the prize still awaits us. The light is sure, but not yet. It is still dawning.

Celebrating the Eucharist encourages us to 'set our minds on what is above... for our life is hidden with Christ in God' *(Colossians 3:2-3)*. At the same time, our longing translates into a desire to make the victory of the Light the reality in our lives. As we connect with our dawn-state, we find that we are called to be 'children of the light and children of the day' *(1 Thessalonians 5:5)*.

For reflection
What meaning do you see in praying at Mass
to be brought to eternal life?

Eucharist is ... Solidarity

'Life is not fair.' There is so much that is not right – poverty, neglect, cruelty, violence, abuse, suffering, discrimination, humiliation ... It would be less than human not to feel disquiet about the human condition.

Amidst all this we celebrate the Eucharist. It is the memorial and perpetuation of Jesus' death on the cross. The death of a young man, innocently executed, his life prematurely ended. His death echoes and amplifies our sense of disquiet.

Remembering his death has been called a 'dangerous memory'. Because it is also to remember all that God remembers in the death of Jesus – the countless millions through the centuries who have suffered innocently and died prematurely. The cross of Jesus communicates to us God's solidarity with these countless millions – their names 'inscribed on the palms of my hands' *(Isaiah 49:16).*

When, before he dies, Jesus says 'Do this in memory of me', what is the 'this' he refers to? 'This' is not just the ritual action, but also what he did during his life, from a heart of divine disquiet. His liberating solidarity with victims, outcast, dispossessed, the poor of the earth, those who suffered innocently. Those of whom he became one in his death – so as to release the power of God's solidarity into the world.

In the Eucharist, our disquiet connects into this divine passion – God's passionate desire that all would be right among God's creatures and in all God's creation. If there isn't this connection, we may well be those whom God addresses with the words, 'I take no delight in your solemn assemblies' *(Amos 5:21)* – because they are rituals without social concern.

Or, as John Paul II put it; 'We cannot delude ourselves: by our mutual love and, in particular, by our concern for those in need we will be recognised as true followers of Christ. This will be the criterion by which the authenticity of our Eucharistic celebrations is judged.'

For reflection
What connection do you find between Eucharist
and justice in the world?

Eucharist is… For Others

There are moments during the Eucharist when our attention is directed outwards. In the Prayer of the Faithful, when we pray for the needs of God's people. Likewise in the intercessions of the Eucharistic Prayer. Again in the Our Father, 'as we forgive those who trespass against us'. Again when we exchange the Sign of Peace. And finally when 'we go in peace to love and serve the Lord'.

This suggests that my participation in the Eucharist isn't just for my own benefit. It is not just 'for me', it is also 'for you'. From this angle, celebrating the Eucharist is an other-centred exercise. We see this very clearly in the many people who go to Mass in order to pray for another – for a friend with troubles, for a son or daughter doing exams, for a neighbour who is ill, for those who have died.

We don't just pray for others; we also thank God for them. Eucharist is about giving thanks – but not only for how I have been blessed. I also give thanks for the blessings of others, for their good fortune, for the grace at work in their lives, for their being a blessing. Rather than grow envious or jealous, I give thanks for all that is good in the lives of those around me.

So, we pray for each other and for the world. And we give thanks for each other and for the world. In this twofold reaching out, we echo the words of Saint Paul about the Body of Christ: 'If one member suffers, all suffer together with it; if one member is honoured, all rejoice together with it.' *(1 Corinthians 12:26)*

But ultimately we echo the words of Jesus at his Last Supper: 'This is my blood of the covenant which is poured out for many.' *(Mark 14:24)* His 'eucharistic prayer' was for many, for others. His final prayer was one of thoughtfulness and his thoughts at death were thoughts for others. In our Eucharistic prayer we are invited to enter into his other-centred spirit.

For reflection
How can I make my participation in the Eucharist
more other-centred?

Four Moments

In this section there are reflections on the four main moments or stages
in the celebration of the Eucharist:

Gathering	82
Word	92
Eucharist	102
Sending	113

For each of these there are two parts:
(a) bringing out the meaning of this part of the Eucharist
(b) presenting possibilities for enhancing the celebration

In relation to (b),
some of the ideas may be familiar, others may be new.
Considering them may in turn generate other ideas.

There is also a reflection/discussion question
with each of the four parts.
These may be particularly useful for liturgy planning groups.

Gathering

A. Reflecting on 'Gathering'

The word 'gathering' refers to the introductory parts of the Mass, up to the beginning of the Liturgy of the Word. Because it is 'introductory', it might not always receive the attention it deserves. Yet it is rich in meaning and possibilities. I think it is no exaggeration to say that, if we grow in appreciation of what 'gathering' is all about, we are on the way to transforming our experience of the Eucharist.

Welcome

Gathering is about welcome and the theme of welcome puts us in touch with something at the very heart of Jesus' own ministry. 'Come to me', he says, 'all you that are weary and carrying heavy burdens, and I will give you rest.' *(Matthew 11:28)* Reflecting on his practice of hospitality helps us see why our gathering at Mass is so significant.

One of the most distinctive aspects of Jesus' life was his practice of sharing table with 'outcasts and sinners', sometimes called his 'table-fellowship'. At the same time, the gospels also depict him as sharing meals with the Pharisees, who are often presented as his opponents. This breadth of table-fellowship with both the so-called sinners and the so-called virtuous accentuates the theme of welcome and inclusivity.

Think for a moment about the 'logic' of his table-fellowship. Those called 'outcasts and sinners' were people who, because of their actions or lifestyle, had been ostracised – for instance, toll-collectors and prostitutes. Now, it is the common human experience that, when others judge or condemn you, or even criticise you, you tend to internalise their attitude and make it your own. Then, as it were, the circle is complete.

Because others did not believe in them, I surmise that many of these people had ceased to believe in themselves. In a very real sense, they had given up on their own future. What Jesus – this charismatic, prophetic figure – does is very simple; he shares table with them. As our own experience of special meals tells us, to share table is to share our lives, our hopes, our selves. It is something of great import in our relationships.

In the case of these people, it was somebody saying to them, 'You are a person; you are noticed; you have a future; you are precious in my eyes.' It was an experience of coming in from the cold, of being liberated, of rediscovering their humanity. It brought joy to their faces again and brought an end to their sadness. There is a tangible sense of people being made happy and their spirits being made free.

But Jesus was not just saying 'in my eyes'. His gesture was saying to them: this is how you are in God's eyes. This is perhaps clearest in the story of the prodigal son. Picture the scene. The son returning, feeling so small, saying 'I am sinner'; the father's arms stretched open in welcome, saying 'You are son.' The son represents each person who feels lost or out in the cold. The father represents the God of Jesus.

So, welcome and hospitality are the heart of the gospel, because they are the heart of God. Jesus shows us that God's heart is a welcoming heart, reaching out to embrace all, so that all might feel that they are noticed, and know that they are welcome, and agree that they are precious.

Church

If this is how God is, the church has no choice. It cannot but reflect God's welcoming heart in all its ways, for 'church' is meant to be a picture of what God is like. Its purpose is to make tangible to people today what those 'outcasts and sinners' felt so immediately. Its purpose is to be a community of people who feel both welcome and called to welcome. Welcoming and feeling welcome should be going on throughout the life of the community – and this is what we link in with at the start of each Mass.

The story of the prodigal son presents us with an image, not just of God, but also of the church. Or rather, two images. On the one hand, the father images a church that is embracing, inviting, welcoming. In contrast, the elder son, however understandable his resentment, images a church that is judgemental, cold-hearted, excluding and exclusive.

The manner of our gathering at Mass has the potential to

symbolise the image of church we that we are trying to live up to. I have noted elsewhere the extent to which parishes today are engaged in forms of outreach that revolve around welcome and belonging and creating a feeling of community.[1] There is a widespread intuition that people 'hear' the good news of the gospel most persuasively when they 'feel' the welcome of the Christian community.

At the same time we all know people who have felt something else. People who have been hurt, people who feel excluded because of the circumstances of their lives or the convictions of their conscience. Like Jesus in the gospels, we know that there are people 'out there' who would be happy if they felt 'called to his supper'.

All this is by way of putting the gathering part of the Eucharist in its wider context. We can grasp the importance of this seemingly inconsequential stage of the ritual when we appreciate the centrality of welcome and belonging to the whole life of the Christian community.

Gathering

'Gathering' is actually the original word for the church. The New Testament word for church is *ekklesia* (as in our 'ecclesiastical'). The ordinary meaning of the word was an assembly, people who have been called together. For the Christians, it meant those who were gathered to celebrate the Eucharist in a particular place.

There is an implication in this that could easily be missed. While the term 'a Christian' may describe your or me as an individual, there is something essentially plural about it! To be a Christian is to be one of those who are gathered. In a sense, 'I am gathered'; I am brought into a Eucharistic community. Being a Christian is personal but it is not private, between 'me and Jesus'. 'Where two or three are gathered in my name, I am there among them.' *(Matthew 18:20)*

If this is so, then *how* we gather is important. How we gather has to reflect how we see ourselves. It is more than 'showing up' or 'turning up', like you might at the dentist's or at a bus stop.

---

1. Donal Harrington, *The Welcoming Parish* (Dublin: Columba, 2005).

There should be a sense of occasion about it. It should in fact itself be an experience of *ecclesia*, an experience of what it is to be 'church'. It should be an experience of the welcoming heart of God.

But this can be hard to achieve. Mass tends to start on time. At two minutes to eleven there may be a scattering of people in the church; at two minutes past the place may be full! There's little time for anything in the way of socialising or 'warming up' – in fact, little or no time for gathering. Contrast this to other meetings, where we may sit or stand around chatting until everybody is present and ready to start.

That means we have to work on it, so that there is a *human* feel to the actual assembling, a feeling of warmth and friendliness, a feeling of hospitality and togetherness, people noticing and being noticed. If there is such a human feel to it, it is more likely that there will be a *divine* feel to it also, a feeling of something special, of God's presence, of God's welcoming embrace.

We could compare it to entering a room, say for a party. There are different ways of entering the room – being greeted warmly and waited upon; arriving unannounced and unnoticed. It does not feel good not to be noticed. It is not pleasant to feel insignificant, or that your presence is of little consequence. Yet we do it all the time at Mass! What does that say about how we see ourselves as 'church' *outside* of Mass?

I remember at Mass one Sunday, I found myself thinking at one point that there is something wrong with all this! I have been sitting here, and while I recognise different faces, I have made no contact with anybody around me. And apart from the sign of peace I will go home with no contact. Little noticing and little being noticed.

I know it is not always like that, but there is a lot of it nonetheless. A young Chinese priest was studying in Dublin a few years ago. He went to different churches each Sunday and his comment after a few months was that on no occasion had he felt a sense of welcome and belonging.[2] Many of us are there as if in a private capacity, for our private devotion. Others are feeling isolated and alone.

2. The story of 'the man with the cap' (above, 'Eucharist is Hospitality') makes the same point.

In contrast to that, there is the practice in many churches, at the start of Mass, of saying a special welcome to those sick or housebound, who are listening in on parish radio. These are people who cannot even be seen by the congregation. They are the most likely not to be noticed at all. Saying a welcome to them is a symbol of what each of those present in the church should be hearing and feeling as well.

It matters how we gather. We want to gather in a way that says we are 'happy to be called to his supper'. We want to gather in a way that makes us feel part of a community of hope and affection.

Baptism

A reflection on baptism is appropriate here. Today it is understood as the sacrament of welcome and belonging. It is a celebration of who I am as a 'new creation in Christ' *(2 Corinthians 5:17)*. But this is more than something interior to me, it is also social. I am 'a citizen with the saints, a member of the household of God' *(Ephesians 2:19)*. To be baptised is to belong.

Part of baptism is the community's commitment to me. It is committed to continuing this experience. It is committed to making people *feel* that they are baptised – partly by making them feel that they belong. In that way, baptism becomes part of my consciousness of who I am, instead of a distant event beyond my earliest memories.

Gathering for the Eucharist should play a big part in the community's commitment to making each person feel they are baptised. Gathering is sacred because we are baptised people, we are gathered people. Baptism means that we are called in out of the cold to share in Jesus' table fellowship, called to be happy.

B. PRACTICAL IDEAS FOR GATHERING

(1)

Welcome begins before we enter the church at all. The environment around the church can communicate a feeling of warmth and welcome. For example, flowers, flower pots, plants give the place a human feel. If there is garden space around the church, the potential for creating a sacred space of quiet could be explored.

The situation of some churches may lend itself to the use of colourful banners or signs outside the church, with a welcoming, inviting message. This is particularly effective for churches located on busy traffic routes. A strong, simple sign could reach thousands of people every day, changing the image of the church from one of lifelessness to one of vibrancy and welcome.

(2)

In a multicultural society, there may be people of many nationalities joining in the Sunday worship. The entry to the church could have a large 'welcome' sign in the different languages of the people who come. Even if the Mass is not in their own language, they will feel noticed. It could lead in turn to their feeling invited to participate in a less anonymous way.

(3)

Lots can be done to create a welcoming environment inside the church building. The quality of the lighting; the heating; the cleanliness; the flower arrangements; the use of banners. All of these 'speak'; they say something about this being a special place, a place of warmth, and about this being a special gathering.

Also, notice-boards that are lively and up to date say something important about us, as a community where things are happening and people are involved. This invites people to stay; whereas notices that are out-of-date can suggest a church that is out of date too. There are all kinds of possibilities – a photo display of recent baptisms; information about parish groups, 'thought for the week', and so on, as well as prayer/reflection leaflets that can help people in their praying.

(4)

More and more parishes are introducing the practice of having people at the church doors to greet people as they arrive. Nothing complicated – just a friendly smile and the Mass leaflet into your hand. It means you do not wait until the sign of peace for a human contact; it is there right at the beginning. Occasionally, somebody moans that they have been coming here for forty years and do not need to be welcomed to their own church. But everybody else really appreciates it – including the person who may have talked to hardly anybody during the past week.

(5)
As well as greeters, there might be ushers to help people find a seat at busy Masses. This was common enough in the past, but it is not just a practical matter. It also changes 'turning up' into 'gathering' and welcome. Also, we do make it hard for latecomers by sitting near the door and sitting at the end of the pew! We might not need ushers at all if we saw a little welcoming ministry here for ourselves.

(6)
There is an idea that relates to the prayer of the faithful later in the celebration (see below in the section on the Liturgy of the Word). To work towards the prayers coming from the faithful, there might be a prayer basket placed at an appropriate location in the church. On arriving, people could write their intention and place it in the basket. Thus, at the start of Mass people would feel that they were bringing their own lives into the liturgy – and that their concerns were welcome here.

(7)
Rather than people just sitting there waiting for the Mass to start, a cantor could go to the lectern and run through some of the music. This would help create a mood and a sense of occasion, as well as encourage people to participate in the singing. In the long-term it would be helping the congregation to develop a repertoire of responses for different parts of the Mass.

(8)
It is well worth considering having an adult or young person to say a few words of welcome before the procession begins. Something very simple, just to give a warm human touch. They might even invite people to say hello to those beside them, again creating a feeling of community. They might also mention the theme of the day's celebration.

Either here, or as part of the priest's own introduction, a welcome to those listening in on parish radio. Whenever this is done at the start of Mass, it gives a strong sense of belonging and thoughtfulness, not just to those listening in, but also to those present in the church.

(9)
There could be an invitation to a quiet moment before Mass begins. This helps to settle people and to make the transition from where they have just come from, into this 'sacred space'. Some people now chat among themselves before Mass and there is no harm in that. But not everybody in the church is equally able to pray quietly and to focus their minds and hearts on what is about to commence.

(10)
Every Mass should begin with a procession to the altar. What the procession does is to draw everybody's attention to the same point, and then to draw everybody into a common focus on the altar. So it has the effect of uniting a collection of individuals into a community of prayer. The procession might include some of those who will minister during the liturgy. It might also include some creative liturgical movement/dance.

(11)
The feeling of welcome and community is increased if there is a lively entrance song that all can join in singing. Three things that could help here: (a) practising the song beforehand; (b) having the words projected onto a large screen; (c) a cantor being part of the procession.

(12)
The priest's own introduction is vital in setting a mood of prayer and fellowship. It is tragic how often the only introduction here is along the lines of; 'Today is the twenty-second Sunday in Ordinary Time' or 'Today's Mass is being offered for ...' There are real possibilities for something far more spiritual and nourishing. The following is an example of the kind of thing the priest could say here:

Let us begin our Mass with a still, quiet moment ...
Lord, let this present moment be as still as a stone
as I rest my heart in you ...

This would be followed by a moment of quiet before leading into the penitential rite. It is very simple, but can have a profound effect of leading people into a special place of prayer.[3]

(13)
The penitential rite, and the way it is introduced, can contribute to the feeling of welcome. Its mood is more a celebration of forgiveness than an examination of conscience. In this way it leads naturally into the Gloria as a song of praise to the God whose mercy we have just confessed.

Besides the penitential prayers being focused on God's mercy, they could also be spoken by a layperson, again adding to the sense of participation. The prayers themselves could be composed locally, perhaps to fit in with the theme of the day.[4]

(14)
There is a lot to be said for more frequent use of the alternative ritual of sprinkling with water to remind us of our baptism. This can be very effective in reminding us, as we gather, of who it is that we are. It helps increase the consciousness of our own baptism as something living and growing. There might be ministers to help in sprinkling the whole congregation.

(15)
There could be a moment of silence before the opening prayer, after the priest says 'Let us pray'. This allows people the space to join their hearts with the sentiment of the prayer. This prayer used to be called the 'Collect' – which has the connotation of gathering our thoughts and focusing them into one prayer.

(16)
Going back to before the celebration commences, is there some-

---

3. See Donal Harrington, *Eucharist: Enhancing the Prayer* (Dublin: Columba, 2007), for a collection of such introductory thoughts.
4. This book also contains texts for the penitential rite.

thing to be said for using the time before Mass for little meetings of parishioners? It can be very hard for people to make it to meetings or gatherings on week nights, but it might be more do-able to come along fifteen or twenty minutes early on Sunday, either for a short prayer experience or for some parish business.

Question for reflection/discussion
Look again at the list of ideas above and ask yourself: what difference would it make if a lot of these things were happening each Sunday?

Word

The Liturgy of the Word is an intrinsic part of the whole celebration, but it is also a unit or a ritual in itself. It includes a first reading usually from the Old Testament, a psalm, a second reading from the New Testament, the gospel acclamation, the gospel reading, the homily, the creed and the prayer of the faithful.

The movement in this is one of listening-connecting-professing-interceding. First, in the readings, we listen and bring to mind the story of salvation. Then, in the homily, we make connections between this, the 'good news', and the realities of our lives. In the creed we profess the faith that unites us in hope. Finally, in the intercessions we transpose the message we have been absorbing into the mode of prayer, for ourselves and for others.

That is the theory, yet it could all amount to quite a succession of 'words words words' – whereas it is in fact meant to be an *experience* of the Word. Lest us reflect, then, on what is meant by 'experiencing the Word', by delving into the deep meaning of this part of the Mass.

The Reality

First, a question: what is the reality when it comes to the Liturgy of the Word? For the average person sitting in the congregation, what is happening during this part of the celebration? Of course, it's a spectrum of different things. One person is seriously engaged, deeply nourished, strongly challenged. Another is 'out of it', making no connection whatsoever. Most of us are somewhere in between. But it might be fair to say that, for a lot of people, not a lot is happening.

One reason for this is a lack of familiarity with the Bible. Historically, Catholics have not been well versed in scripture. Even priests in the past received little education in the Bible. I remember, when I was growing up, there was a big ornate Bible in the house, in a box that was never opened. There was even a certain unease with reading scripture. One priest tells the story, from around 1960 or so, of a parishioner asking him for permission to buy a Bible!

Things are changing now, but changing a culture is a slow process. So, listening to scripture at Mass still feels more remote than homely for many people. This is especially true of the Old Testament, but it applies to all the readings to some degree. They do not echo, resonate, strike a chord as they should. They do not engage, surprise, transform as they are meant to.

In addition, the quality of the proclamation varies greatly. At its best, it can help make accessible what is strange and unfamiliar. At its worst, it doubles the difficulty; bad enough the content being strange when you cannot even hear it properly.

More than Words

A huge shift has taken place in our understanding of the Word of God at Mass. It originated with the Vatican Council and is captured in the following passage from one of its documents:

> The church has always venerated the divine scriptures just as she venerates the body of the Lord, since, especially in the sacred liturgy, she unceasingly receives and offers to the faithful the bread of life from the table both of God's word and of Christ's body.

This is almost revolutionary! The Word of God and the Body of Christ are on the same footing. In the Word of God we receive the bread of life. The Word is more than words: it is life, the bread of life. It is the Word made flesh. It is not a prelude to the real thing. When we hear 'This is the word of the Lord', it is the event itself, just as when we hear 'This is the body of Christ'. His presence is no less real.

God's Word is powerful. From the very first words of creation, God's Word carries the power of God's Spirit; it makes things happen. 'God said, let there be light; and there was light'. (Genesis 1:3) There is a quality about God's Word that makes it unique, greater than any human word.

God is not a human being, that he should lie,
or a mortal, that he should change his mind.
Has he promised and will he not do it?
Has he spoken and will he not fulfil it? *(Numbers 23:19)*

When God's Word is spoken, God is active. When God's Word is spoken something is happening. We see this clearly in a phrase from later in the Mass, when we echo the words of the centurion in the gospels: 'Only say the word and I shall be healed.'

Because of this, the Liturgy of the Word is more aptly described in terms of 'proclaiming' than of 'reading'. 'Reading the reading' sounds the same as 'reading the notices'; it is just saying something. 'Proclaiming the Word', in contrast, has the feeling of an event. If we engage with a listening heart, we don't just hear something. God's Word does something to us.

The Broader Picture

But this needs to be seen in the broader context of our daily Christian living. The Word at Mass is not like an oasis in the desert, unlike anything else around. The Word we hear is also the Word that is at the heart of our daily Christian existence.

The Word is at the heart of life because each of us is a 'fifth gospel'. Each of the four gospels tells the story of the good news in a different way, from a different perspective. Similarly, each follower of Christ today tells the story through the medium of who they are and how they live. We are all, each in our own way, a new version of the good news.

In the same vein, Francis de Sales said: 'There is no more difference between the written gospels and the lives of saints than between written music and music sung.' We are those 'saints', in whose lives the words of the gospel come to life. When we live Christian lives, the Word can be seen and heard. It takes flesh once again.

To be a Christian is to have this amazing, intimate relationship with the Word of God. So we can appreciate what Saint Peter means when he says:

> You have been born anew, not of perishable, but of imperishable seed through the living and enduring word of God ... That word is the good news that was announced to you. *(1 Peter 1:23, 25)*

As followers of Christ, we are born again. The Word of the gospel has given birth to each of us as a new creation. In it is contained our 'programme' for living. The lives we lead, and not just the readings at Mass, are meant to be a proclamation of the Word.

Listening to the Word

From this broader context of our lives we can see that listening to scripture at Mass is something akin to looking at ourselves in a mirror. When we hear the words, it is like being told who we are. It is like the woman in the gospels who says to her people about Jesus, 'Come and see a man who told me everything I have ever done!' *(John 4:29)* In the Word we encounter Jesus and in meeting Jesus we encounter the innermost truth about ourselves.

This makes listening to the Word a sacred event, just as the words of Jesus at the consecration are sacred. Caesarius of Arles, from the sixth century, expresses eloquently the kind of respect this entails:

> Brothers and sisters, here is a question for you: which to you seems the greater, the Word of God or the Body of Christ? If you want to give the right answer, you will reply that God's Word is not less than Christ's Body. Therefore, just as we take care when we receive the Body of Christ so that no part of it falls to the ground so, likewise, should we ensure that the Word of God which is given to us is not lost to our souls because we are speaking or thinking about something different. One who listens negligently to God's Word is just as guilty as one who, through carelessness, allows Christ's Body to fall to the ground.

When we listen, we do so with an awareness of the power within the words. We listen with the heart. We listen with a sense of anticipation of the Word being made flesh and Christ becoming truly present.

And our listening is not confined to our time at Mass. If we are born of the Word, then we live our lives in constant reference to the Word. We take it with us wherever we go. We give quality time to reading scripture. We find ways to extend our listening beyond Mass, to hear Christ speak in countless different ways throughout the day.

The One who Speaks

We are used to speaking of 'Readers' and of 'Ministers of the Eucharist'. Even the terms suggest a difference of status. Indeed, many readers would feel that theirs is not quite as important a ministry. The foregoing perspectives should correct that misapprehension. When the reader speaks, it is Christ whom we hear. As Saint Augustine put it: 'The reader goes to the lectern, but it is Christ who is not silent.'

The title 'Minister of the Word' would reflect this better than 'Reader'. It gets us to the heart of what is going on. It is far more than 'reading the reading'. It is even more than 'proclaiming the Word'. It is, in fact, the ministry of facilitating the action of the word in those who are listening. Each of us is called to proclaim the gospel with the lives we lead, to lead lives rooted in the Word from which we have been born anew. The minister of the Word at Mass is at the service of this, a midwife to each of us becoming what we are meant to be – 'a fifth gospel'.

B. Practical Ideas for the Liturgy of the Word

(1)

Sometimes there is a strong theme running through the readings. In that case it may be worth highlighting the theme at the beginning of Mass, choosing music that links in with it, composing penitential prayers around it, picking it up in the homily and referring to it again in the prayers of the faithful. That gives a unity to the whole liturgy of the Word, and the possibility for a focused and sustained reflection on the part of the congregation.

(2)

Many people feel that three readings is too much to digest, especially when texts are unfamiliar and hard to comprehend. While there are different views on this, it might be worth considering a reduction, for the sake of the overall effect. There is a logic to the three-year structure of readings, but perhaps a more important issue is that people have a welcoming rather than alienating experience of the Word of God.

Since there is a thematic link between the Old Testament and gospel readings, the New Testament reading might be the one to move. On the other hand, it may often be the one that is easier to relate to. One possibility, when reducing, is to use a thought from one of the readings elsewhere in the Mass, for instance as a reflection after communion. In that way its message is not being lost.

(3)

A focused introduction can help make the readings more welcoming. By 'focused' I mean something very brief that directs people towards some theme to look out for in the readings. This is especially useful when the meaning of the texts is more abstruse. Then people are not being left to grapple on their own. They may even feel more encouraged to put in an effort.

(4)

Alternatively, one could begin with a quiet moment to focus attention. Silence is a very important element of the liturgy of the Word. It creates a mood of meditation where people can absorb what God is saying into their hearts. For example, the priest could say something like the following (drawing on the psalms), followed by a very brief pause:

We listen now to the Word of God and we pray:
'My soul waits for your word, O Lord, and in your word I hope.'

(5)

Another moment[5] when silence is appropriate is at the end of the homily, to help people formulate a message for themselves. The priest could say something like this:

Before moving on, we'll have a quiet moment to think –
what is the Lord saying to me today?

The Liturgy of the Word can be a flood of words – reading, psalm, reading, gospel, homily. The 'soil' of my heart needs time and calm to soak up the rich nourishment. It cannot be rushed.

(6)

Besides silence, music is a key part of making the liturgy of the

---

5. There are more texts for both these moments in *Eucharist: Enhancing the Prayer*.

Word meditative and prayerful. Ideally, all would sing the response to the psalm (itself a response to the first reading) and the gospel acclamation. It would be good for the congregation to learn a simple repertoire of responses to suit different moods and themes and seasons. As well, going back-and-forth between reading and singing also dispels the sense of 'words words words'.

(7)
During the gospel acclamation, there might occasionally be a simple procession with the book of the gospels. This helps highlight the presence of Christ in the Word, as well as focus people's eyes and hearts on the gospel to be proclaimed.

(8)
There are possibilities for enhancing the quality of the homily. These deserve serious consideration because of the potential impact of this part of the Mass on people. I am thinking in particular of the burden on the priest of producing quality material every Sunday – often speaking to the same people week in, week out.

In some places, priests from neighbouring parishes meet to pray about and discuss the Scripture readings for the following weekend. In other places, a group meets during the week in the parish, for a *lectio divina* style sharing on the gospel. In these ways, the priest's homily is enriched by the thoughts and experience of others.

We know how effective it can be also to have other voices occasionally. A mother sharing her experience on an Advent Sunday ... On another occasion somebody sharing their reflections on illness or disability ... On another, somebody from the pastoral council, or the Vincent de Paul ... Without in any way taking from the priest's role, there is also something invaluable about the witness of lay people hearing lay people speak during the Eucharist.

There is also potential in an occasional shared homily. The priest and the other person could structure the presentation in a question-and-answer format. The 'other person' might, for instance, have a particular experience to relate, such as their time ministering abroad. Or it might simply be a parishioner with whom the priest teases out the application of the day's gospel. This format has proved to be quite engaging.

(9)

There are options for the Creed also. We already have a choice between the Nicence Creed, the shorter Apostles' Creed, and the renewal of baptism promises. The latter, with its question-and-answer format, could be used more often to forge a link in people's minds between the creed and their own baptism. Indeed, the earliest creeds we have (in the New Testament) come from the baptism ceremony.

The 'Glory be …' could also be used as a very short profession of faith. A creative option would be to compose a creed, perhaps in relation to a particular occasion or theme, perhaps in the same question-answer format as the baptism renewal.

(10)

The prayer of the faithful would ideally be just that – the prayers coming from the people present. Given that this is not usually feasible, there could be a prayer basket in the aisle. People could put in their intentions, the basket could be brought up at this point, and possibly one or two petitions read out. This could help people feel that their concerns are included in the prayers.

I think that the prayers of the faithful should be brief, with no more than four or five of them. Prayers that go on and on are counter-productive. I suggest that they should be a balance of prayers reflecting the themes of the readings and prayers reflecting what is topical or local.[6]

In a way, the prayers are harder to get across than the readings. Precisely because they are so brief, they can be lost if they are not enunciated well. They deserve to be proclaimed in a way that draws people into their sentiments. Alternating voices (male-female?) can help capture attention. Singing the response can allow the intention of the prayer to sink in.

A question that might be asked: are the prayers of the faithful

6. *Eucharist: Enhancing the Prayer* contains prayers of the faithful that are built from the scripture readings, for each Sunday of the three-year cycle.

that we have prepared for this Mass worthy of being included in the weekly bulletin or newsletter? If they were composed with care, reflecting both the scripture and what is going on in the world, people might benefit from being able to take them home.

(11)

The parish needs to attend seriously to the quality of the proclamation in the liturgy of the Word. In one parish, the ministers of the Word themselves met and composed their own list of do's and don'ts (e.g. read slowly, prepare beforehand, etc.) as a kind of 'commitment to quality'. Some parishes have brought the ministers together in small groups, to be recorded and then to watch the video and give each other feedback. Some have explored the idea of each minister having a 'mentor' to give them ongoing feedback.

Some parishes have discovered the value of a couple of gatherings each year to enrich the ministers in their spirituality and their appreciation of scripture. Some also provide resource material – background reading, commentaries, missals, etc. Part of the ongoing renewal might be an annual rededication of ministers of the Word (and commissioning of new ones) at homily time. This also serves as a consciousness-raising for the whole congregation about the Word of God.

(12)

The parish website has a part to play also. The readings for the following Sunday can be signalled for those who would like to read them in advance. The text of the previous weekend's homily and/or prayers could be made available.

(13)

On a broader front, whatever helps people generally to grow in their knowledge and love of scripture is going to feed into the quality of how the liturgy of the Word is experienced. Reflections in the newsletter, encouraging the reading of the Bible, making Bibles (or individual books) available, a *lectio divina* group, a scripture study group – all of these help move us in the direction of being a people whose Christian lives are deeply rooted in the living Word.

Perhaps there is work here for the Ministers of the Word. If they were meeting for enrichment occasionally during the year, they might begin to see a ministry for themselves beyond the Eucharist. They might see that they have a role in initiating the kind of ventures mentioned in the last paragraph. That would be a realisation of their ministry of facilitating each member of the Body in becoming a 'fifth gospel'.

If these kinds of suggestions were being implemented, the role of the missalette might come in for review. Often, as somebody said, it can 'sit like a great wall of ice between the reader and the assembly'.

But if the reader is proclaiming, and if proclaiming is the event of God speaking to us, then the assembly's role is the more active one of looking up and listening. The missalette, in turn, takes on the role of an aid, to prepare with beforehand and to return to after the proclamation.

Question for reflection/discussion
Which of the ideas above do you think have the greatest potential
to transform people's experience of the Liturgy of the Word?

Eucharist

A. REFLECTING ON 'EUCHARIST'

The Liturgy of the Eucharist begins with the presentation of the gifts. This leads into the heart of the celebration, the Eucharistic Prayer. This is followed by the Communion Rite, beginning with the Our Father and culminating in communion.

The different Eucharist Prayers follow the same structure. This includes (a) a moment of thanksgiving; (b) calling on the Holy Spirit; (c) the Last Supper narrative (consecration); (d) remembering what God has done for us in Christ; (d) prayers to God, to accept the offering, for the church and the world, and for the dead.

Throughout, the focus is on what God has done for us in Christ. In the Eucharist, this is a present and continuing reality; what happened then is happening now. As in the Liturgy of the Word, the words being spoken are filled with the power of what God is doing among us.

Whose action?

What God is doing is obviously the heart of it. And while we are all participants, people might be forgiven for seeing this part of the Mass, especially the Eucharistic Prayer, as 'the priest's bit'.

Elsewhere in the liturgy there seems to be much more scope for 'audience participation' – greeters, ministers of the Word, those presenting the gifts, ministers of the Eucharist, and so on. But the Eucharistic Prayer is where the priest comes more to centre stage. Apart from some sung and spoken responses, the congregation appears to be in a largely passive mode.

In our understanding of the Eucharist, this may be where the biggest mind shift of all is required. We are coming out of a long period of history where the Mass was something that happened up on the altar, at the hands of the priest, with the congregation looking on from a distance. The cultural conditioning dissolves slowly, as we learn to appreciate that what is going on at this part of the Mass is the action of all of us.

I remember somebody capturing this in a rather striking way, as follows. In both the Liturgy of the Word and the Liturgy of the Eucharist, there is listening taking place, but it is a different kind of listening in each case. In the Liturgy of the Word, God is speaking to us and we are actively listening, waiting to hear God's Word in the words being proclaimed.

In the Liturgy of the Eucharist it is God who is listening. And it is us – *all of us* – that God is listening to. In the Eucharistic Prayer, the whole gathering speaks, *through* the priest. As one church document puts it, it is a prayer that the priest addresses in the name of the entire community to God. He speaks on behalf of all; when he speaks, all of us are speaking.

In a very real sense this means that we are all co-celebrants. We are not onlookers but active participants. This is why we now speak of the priest 'presiding' rather than 'saying Mass'. To speak of him presiding indicates that he is gathering and articulating the prayer of all the people.

From this perspective the term 'con-celebration' can be misleading. The post-Vatican II practice of priests concelebrating supplanted the older practice of different priests saying their own Masses at different altars. However, it may have the effect of reinforcing the impression that it is *only* the priests who are 'doing something'.

When we gather, it is to do something together. What is it that we do? It could be described in different ways, but in what follows I have chosen to focus on just three ways of expressing it. What we do is to give thanks, to offer sacrifice, and to break bread.

Giving thanks

'Eucharist' is a Greek word meaning thanksgiving and it became the main word for the Mass from very early on, with the heart of the ritual being the prayer of thanks over the bread and wine. If today it is again the favoured word for the celebration, that puts the theme of giving thanks right to the fore. Eucharist means that we gather together to give thanks.

'Thanks' is intimately linked to 'grace'. Indeed the Greek word for grace – *charis* – is the core of the word 'Eucharist'. But what is grace? I like this reflection as quoted from the singer Bruce Springsteen:

We live in a tragic world, but there's grace all around you. That's tangible. So you try to attend to the grace. That's how I try to guide myself – and our house, the kids. Grace to me, it's just the events of the day. The living breath of our lives … So you're chauffeuring your kids somewhere and you think it's a burden and something happens … it's there.

In the same vein, an Irish theologian wrote a book once called *Life and Grace*. Years later he was said to have remarked that, were he writing it now, he would change the title to *Life is Grace*. From the Christian point of view, being fully human is very much about seeing life as grace.

Experiencing life as grace flows naturally into an attitude of thankfulness. But it is not automatic. I am thinking of the story of the ten lepers. All experienced healing and I presume all were filled with joy. But it is one thing to experience the gift, another to acknowledge the giver. One of the ten took that step and went back to Jesus to express thanks.

That is what 'Eucharist' is. We return to the source of the grace, to remember the giver of the gift. You do not have to be a believer to experience life as grace (though you will hardly use that language). But perhaps what is distinctive about faith is its recognition of the giver of the gift, its revelation as to who that giver is.

And so the Eucharistic Prayer begins with a dialogue of thanks: 'Lift up your hearts/We lift them up to the Lord; Let us give thanks to the Lord our God/It is right to give him thanks and praise.'

The theme of thanks and praise continues in the opening words of the different Eucharistic Prayers: 'We come to you Father with praise and thanksgiving'; 'It is our duty and salvation always and everywhere to give you thanks'; 'You are holy indeed and all creation rightly gives you praise'; 'Father in heaven it is right that we should give you thanks and praise.'

It is all leading up to Jesus' own words of thanks: 'He took bread and gave you thanks … he took the cup. Again he gave you thanks and praise.' In the apparent tragedy of his life, ended abruptly, innocently and violently, he gives thanks. Even there, life is grace. Inspired by him, and in imitation of him, we give thanks – not because our lives have been lucky, but because they are blessed.

If we are giving thanks, in a way it does not seem natural to stay silent! At least the dialogue quoted above, the 'Holy, holy', and the consecration acclamation allow us to give voice to our gratitude. Maybe also there should be a space for people to ponder, and possibly express what they are thankful for.

Offering sacrifice
In the first millennium there was a distancing of the people from the Mass – Latin no longer their spoken language; the altar area separated off from where the people sat; the Eucharistic prayer said silently; communion received rarely and on the tongue. What was happening was happening 'up there' and not 'down here', a spectacle almost, to be watched with awe.

This deeply affects our feeling for the Mass as 'sacrifice'. Sacrifice can have three meanings – Jesus' giving of his life on the Cross; the perpetuation of this in the Eucharist; and the Christian's self-giving or sacrifice of self. The latter got lost, and with it a vital connection between 'up there' and 'down here'.

And yet, in our Mass today, these interlinked meanings of sacrifice are waiting to be found. It begins with the presentation of the gifts. However, this sometimes amounts to no more than the bread and wine being moved from a side-table to the altar, rather like 'laying the table'. Sometimes they may be on the altar already, so that there is no 'presentation' at all.

In the early church, it seems that people brought gifts with them to the Eucharist. Some of the bread brought was blessed and broken for that occasion. Some of what was brought was collected for distribution to the poor. There is a strong element of *giving* in this: both the 'material' for the celebration coming from the people, and the solidarity with others in need.

The old word 'offertory' conveys something of this, that we are offering ourselves, in a sense putting ourselves on the table of the Lord. Likewise the words of the hymn: 'In bread we bring you, Lord, our bodies' labour; in wine we offer you our spirits' grief.' We are up there with the bread and wine. In a very real way they represent us.

So, as we watch with the eyes of our bodies the bread and

wine being brought forward, what we see with the eyes of our hearts is ourselves being presented – our tears and tensions, all the desire and love that is in us. We do not leave our lives in the porch as if this has nothing to do with us. Not just bread and wine to be changed, but also ourselves to be transformed.

This is stated with great strength and clarity in the third Eucharistic Prayer. Before the consecration we hear: 'And so Father, we bring you these gifts. We ask you to make them holy by the power of your Spirit, that they may become the body and blood of your Son ...' And after the consecration: 'Grant that we, who are nourished by his body and blood, may be filled with the Holy Spirit and become one body, one spirit in Christ. May he make us an everlasting gift to you.'

First, 'that they may become'; then, 'that we may become'. The meanings of 'sacrifice' are indeed interlinked. The linking factor is the Holy Spirit. We call on the Spirit to make Jesus present in the bread and wine. We then call on the Spirit to change us into the Body of Christ. Two realities converge into one – the bread that is Jesus our life; the bread that is us, his body.

So we are all 'priests' – a word, in its ancient meaning, closely bound up with sacrifice. We see the consecration very clearly related to the priesthood of the ordained, but less obviously related to the priesthood of all believers (1 Peter 2:5, 9). Less obvious but no less real; for by baptism we are all 'ordained' to offer sacrifice, called in the words of Saint Paul, 'to present your bodies as a living sacrifice, holy and acceptable to God, which is your spiritual worship.' (Romans 12:1)

'Sacrifice' – sacrum facere – means to make holy. We are part of what is being made holy. We offer ourselves. We are part of the mystery. We are precious; we are changed. In the self-sacrificing love of Jesus, present on the altar, we see mirrored our own self-sacrificing love also, our love transformed and taken up into his.

Breaking bread

'The breaking of bread', together with 'The Lord's Supper', is probably the oldest term for our gathering.[7] According to the

7. See Acts 2:42, 46: 20:7, 11 (breaking of bread); 1 Corinthians 11:20 (Lord's supper).

Catechism, what the first Christians meant by this term was that 'all who eat the one broken bread, Christ, enter into communion with him and form but one body in him'.

Again, what is described is something that *we do*. Some of the language we have used obscures this. We are used to saying that bread and wine are changed into the body and blood of Christ, and that we then 'receive' communion. A change takes place on the altar and what is changed is then given to us – little or no activity on our part. It is an incomplete perspective.

What is needed here is an interlinking of different meanings of 'bread/body', similar to the different meanings of 'sacrifice' above. Bread/body may refer to Jesus in his life on earth, his body broken on the Cross, his giving himself as the bread of life. They may refer to the bread placed on the altar, to be transformed into the risen Christ. And they may refer to us, the Body of Christ.

Again, our history has been one of losing sight of the third meaning. We have spoken of the body of Christ on the altar in a way that we have not spoken of the body of Christ in the pews. So much so that we lost sight of the peculiarity of the term 'receiving communion'. Properly speaking, communion is not something we receive; it is something we enter into. It is not some kind of item or commodity. It is the reality of what we become.

It could be expressed as follows: what we receive *is* what we become. Communion with Jesus, and communion with one another as his body, are intimately one. John Paul II put it thus:

> Receiving the Eucharist means entering into a profound communion with Jesus. This cannot be adequately understood or fully experienced apart from communion among Christians themselves ... we walk with Christ to the extent that we are in relationship with his body.

Probably the most eloquent expression of this is the sermon of Saint Augustine quoted earlier.[8] When the minister says 'Body of Christ' and we respond 'Amen', we are saying 'yes' to what we are. Augustine concludes by exhorting us to live as Christ's body, so that our Amen may be true.

8. See above, 'Eucharist is ... The Body of Christ'.

This is the background for appreciating 'the breaking of bread'. The actual breaking of bread by the priest may hardly be noticed, and there are already hundreds of separate other pieces ready for distribution. Yet this inadequate symbolism is meant to carry the truth of 'one bread one body': that bread broken is bread shared and bread shared is a communion in the body of Christ.

Seeing Eucharist as the breaking of bread takes us beyond private devotion and into the sphere of shared action. As with a significant meal, where we also 'break bread', we come together to be together and to do something together. In doing that something – the breaking of bread – we become what it signifies.

We give thanks; we offer sacrifice; we break bread. In the Eucharist we are doing something together, and in our shared action God is doing something to us. The ideas that follow are mainly on the theme of the Eucharist being our shared action, and on how that can be brought out more effectively in our celebration.

B. Practical Ideas for the Liturgy of the Eucharist

(1)

At the presentation of the gifts, it is good to highlight our giving of ourselves. It is a time to build a stronger sense in people that we are more than onlookers; that, in the words of Augustine quoted earlier, it is our own mystery that is being placed on the table of the Lord.

This can be achieved by having a simple spoken reflection as the gifts are being brought forward.[9] At the same time, something special can be made of the procession with the gifts, through music and/or liturgical movement.

(2)

Those presenting the gifts might themselves place them on the altar themselves, as a way of reinforcing the sense that we place ourselves on the altar. Handing them to the priest and servers at the steps to the sanctuary can suggest that we do not belong in the sacred place.

---

9. See texts in *Eucharist: Enhancing the Prayer*.

(3)

This can be combined with members of the congregation dressing the altar. That means leaving it bare until this time. And keeping it simple – a cloth, the bread and wine, the book – strengthens the focus. Sometimes there is so much clutter that the bread and chalice are hidden from sight. Flowers and candles can be arranged in a way that does not obscure the central focus.

(4)

It is worth taking the opportunities that present themselves for emphasising the themes of self-giving and solidarity in the collection. The collection can seem to be just a fact of life, an unavoidable necessity that has to be included. Originally, as we said above, it was more than this and included bringing food for the poor. Today, most collections are for the support of the clergy.

However, there are a number of occasions during the year when it is possible to highlight self-giving. There are the annual collection for the Vincent de Paul Society, occasional collections for humanitarian disasters, and other opportunities. These are times to put into words that a part of our coming together for Eucharist is to express our solidarity with the poor.

(5)

As in the other parts of the Mass, space should be made for silence. This can be done, for instance, at the start of the Eucharistic Prayer, or at the Our Father, or before the Sign of Peace, or after Communion.[10] The silence need only be very brief, just a focused moment to heighten attention. This has the effect of creating a mood of silence that permeates the surrounding prayer and ritual.

One example: since the Eucharistic Prayer is a prayer of thanksgiving, it could begin with an invitation to quietly reflect on what we are thankful for. This makes for a mood of thankful participation in what follows.

(6)

We could avail more of all the options when it comes to choos-

---

10. See texts in *Eucharist: Enhancing the Prayer*.

ing the Eucharistic Prayer. Pre-printed leaflets can be restrictive here. Besides the four most frequently used prayers, there are two on the theme of reconciliation, three for children and four more for various needs and occasions. That is thirteen 'official' prayers in all.

Many people find the language of the Eucharistic Prayer difficult and uninviting. This may actually be more true of some of the prayers we use most frequently. If so, it reinforces the case for availing of all the options. Some of the less familiar prayers – including, but not only the prayers for children – are expressed in more accessible language.

(7)

Everything possible deserves to be done to maximise participation and to move people out of an 'onlooker' mode. The dialogue in the children's Eucharistic Prayer is a good example. We could make a priority of everybody joining together in singing the Holy holy, the Proclamation of Faith and the Great Amen.

I suspect that there is an impetus in the congregation towards more participation. We have seen how people join in saying 'Through him, with him, in him' and in the Peace prayer (sometimes despite being discouraged). Were they invited, I think people might quite readily join in the whole Eucharistic Prayer! Meanwhile, they could be encouraged to say the words silently with the priest. He is, after all, speaking on behalf of the whole gathering.

(8)

People could be invited to join hands for the Our Father. It may feel awkward, but children have no problem with it! Maybe it is something to work towards, as a symbol of communion and our engaging in a shared action.

(9)

More parishes are trying to approximate as nearly as possible to the symbolism of 'one bread one body'. Even if it is not feasible to break one bread among so many, there could be one large bread on the altar. Along with this, all the bread for this Mass should be brought up in the presentation of the gifts. Anything else reduces the imagery of our being the body of Christ.

(10)
It is beginning to become the norm that people receive from the cup also at communion time. As it stands, the cup is a negligible part of most people's sense of communion. So, it has to be introduced with care, occasionally then more frequently, with good catechesis and lots of encouragement (including for the Ministers of the Eucharist).

(11)
We should pay attention to making communion time as welcoming and inclusive as possible. Firstly, we can invite parents to bring pre-communion children forward for a blessing from the minister. Likewise, adults who (for whatever reason) are not receiving can be invited to approach with their arms crossed, for a blessing.

(12)
As with the Ministers of the Word, we need to take good care of the Ministers of the Eucharist. Usually they are not so much a group (like a choir, for instance) as a collection of individuals. It is possible for it to become a routine, performing a task rather than practising a ministry. Unless deliberate attention is paid, at least some may drift into this mode.

There might be occasional meetings during the year. These could be devoted to enriching people's spirituality, as well as to considering ways of developing the ministry. One development might be to introduce receiving from the chalice. Another might be for Ministers to bring communion from Mass to those who are housebound. Another might be to take on the related ministry of hospitality, greeting people as they come to church, thereby building the sense of 'the body'.

There might also be an annual rededication of existing ministers and commissioning of new ones. Part of the value of this is its potential as a catechetical moment for the community at large, in its appreciation of itself as the Body of Christ.

(13)

The time after communion presents another opportunity for quiet, but it may need to be structured in order to be effective. The more efficiently communion is completed, with more rather than less ministers, the more space is created for this quiet. While a good communion reflection can help, a few simple words to focus a time of silent prayer, perhaps with instrumental music, may be even more valuable.

It might sound strange to suggest also the possibility of everybody together singing a verse or two of a song or hymn, led by a cantor. If the song is a kind of meditative chant, and if all are joining in, an unusually powerful sense of quiet can be created.

Question for reflection/discussion
What possibilities do you see in the above for leading people
to a more active participation in the Liturgy of the Eucharist?

Sending

A. REFLECTING ON 'SENDING'

It might appear unbalanced to see the concluding rites as one of the main parts of the Mass. It is so very brief, being little more than the blessing and dismissal of the congregation. But there is much more to it than might appear at first sight.

This is what the title 'sending' is intended to convey. While 'concluding rites' suggests an ending, 'sending' suggests a continuation, even a beginning. Recall how 'gathering' is far more than just turning up or starting off, but is full of the meaning of what we are as church. So 'sending' is far more than 'ending'. It too is deeply expressive of who we are.

Drawn inwards – impelled outwards
Earlier I referred to a reflection of John Paul II about this part of the Mass. He was speaking of how Matthew, Mark and Luke have similar accounts of Jesus sharing the bread and wine at the Last Supper, whereas John has no such account:

> It is not by chance that the gospel of John contains no account of the institution of the Eucharist, but instead relates the washing of feet; by bending down to wash the feet of his disciples, Jesus explains the meaning of the Eucharist unequivocally.

This is an arresting thought: the washing of feet is the meaning of the Eucharist! It is not sufficient to say that bread and wine are about Eucharist and that washing of feet is about service – a kind of 'liturgy and life' couple. Of course that is so, but it misses a key part of the reason why John chooses this narrative instead of what the other three gospels recount. How, then, does the washing of feet so clearly explain the Eucharist?

In his two actions at the Last Supper Jesus, as it were, gathers up all that he lived for and stood for. In washing the disciples' feet, he is saying that life for him is all about the gracious giving and receiving of ministry. By including this story in his gospel,

John is clarifying for us that Eucharist is all about this too. In other words, the Eucharist is about *God washing our feet*. It is not quite the case that we have Eucharist (bread and wine) now and service (washing of feet) later. Rather, the Eucharist *is* service, God's ministering to us in this gracious act of hospitality. The washing of feet, like the bread and wine, symbolises God's gift of God's own self to us.

This means that Eucharist is an invitation to allow ourselves to be ministered to. This is the issue in Peter's resisting when Jesus would wash his feet. Jesus says, 'If you do not let me, you can have no part with me.' We receive a share in divine grace by allowing God to give. Thus the Eucharist represents the basic commandment of Christianity: allow yourself to be loved.

In physics there is the concept of 'centripetal' and 'centrifugal' forces. A centripetal force draws something inwards towards the centre; a centrifugal force pushes it outwards, away from the centre. This provides a thought-provoking image with which to consider the twofold dynamism of the Eucharist.

On the one hand, there is its 'centripetal' force. This is our being drawn in towards the centre, inwards toward God's love for us in Jesus. But this is matched by its centrifugal force, which is God's sending us forth. Jesus goes on to say to Peter and the others: 'As I have washed your feet so you also ought to wash one another's feet.' We share in divine grace by extending the experience beyond the celebration. God's service to us is not to be separated from our mutual service.

Sending
If the concluding rite – such a small fraction of the ritual – were passed over in a cursory way, this connection could be lost. This is all the more important in that the Eucharist can easily be experienced in a self-referenced kind of manner. It can be experienced as 'special time for me', 'uplifting', 'nourishing'. When it is this and no more, it is centripetal without being centrifugal.

This danger may be even greater in today's context. Alongside all the great things happening 'spirituality' today, there are worrying trends, one of which is a consumerist interpretation of spirituality. In the capitalist culture we are consumers. We go to the shopping mall, acquire what we desire and bring it home to enjoy. Likewise, if we are so inclined, we go to church to acquire. We are in receiving mode, 'for me'.

The thrust of the gospel experience is so different. There is a pattern in people's encounters with Jesus that reflects the centripetal-centrifugal imagery. It is a pattern of receiving *and* giving, of being graced *and* called to be grace in turn, of being ministered to by Jesus *and* then being missioned by him – of having our feet washed by him *and* being sent to wash each other's feet in turn.

For example, John (chapter four) narrates the Samaritan woman's encounter with Jesus. Through the encounter she is truly enlightened, about herself, about God, about life. But the experience leads her back to her city, to tell others about what had happened, so that 'many Samaritans from that city believed in him because of the woman's testimony'. Receiving and giving, being ministered to by Jesus flows into mission.

Again, Mark's gospel (chapter five) tells the story of a man possessed by demons, who is healed and liberated in dramatic fashion by Jesus. The man begs to go with Jesus, but Jesus tells him instead to 'Go home to your friends and tell them how much the Lord has done for you and what mercy he has shown you.' Spiritual experiences can leave you just wanting more, but for Jesus they lead to mission.

Again, Luke (chapter seven) recounts the incident of the woman washing Jesus' feet with her tears and drying them with her hair and kissing them with her lips and anointing them with ointment. This views the same dynamic from the other end. As Jesus explains her action, such an overflow of love from her heart has its source in the forgiveness she has experienced. God has washed her feet; now she ministers in turn.

This pattern in the gospels is the pattern in the Eucharist. As John Paul II put it, 'Once we have truly met the Risen One by partaking of his body and blood, we cannot keep to ourselves the joy we have experienced.' That captures so well how it must have felt for those three people; it is meant to be our experience also. Drawn inwards, we experience an indescribable joy; impelled outwards, it is a joy that cannot be contained.

Receiving flows into giving; that is the natural thrust of the experience. Eucharist has to link with life; it is not entire in itself.

As somebody put it, 'when the service is over, the real service begins'.

Mass

So central is the 'sending' theme that it is contained in our traditional word for the sacrament, the 'Mass'. As noted earlier, 'Mass' comes from the Latin word for sending – *mitto/missum* – which is also the source of our word 'mission'. At the end of the Latin Mass, the priest said, *Ite, missa est* – 'Go, it is the dismissal'. It was a form of dismissal, but it has the rich suggestion of Mass being completed in mission. John Paul II said:

> The dismissal at the end of each Mass is a charge given to Christians, inviting them to work for the spread of the gospel and the imbuing of society with Christian values.

The 'mission', of course, is not ours but God's. In theology, mission is originally a word pertaining to the Trinity – the Father sending the Son, then the sending of the Spirit through Jesus' death and resurrection. Only then is it our sending: 'As the Father has sent me, so I send you.' *(John 20:21)* Our Christian lives are born out of mission, God's mission to us, which we celebrate in the Eucharist, which is completed in turn by our continuing God's mission in the world.

God washes our feet – only complete when we serve each other. Bread broken for us – only complete when we are bread broken for one another. Body of Christ which we receive – only complete as we become the Body of Christ. Christ's sacrifice for us – only complete in the living sacrifice of our lives. Giving thanks to God – only complete in living thankful lives.

What is at stake here is no less than the authenticity of our celebration. A genuine celebration has happened when Mass becomes mission.

Ministry

The intimate link between Eucharist and service is already to be seen in the ministries at work within the celebration. There is quite a variety – the one who greets at the door, the altar servers, the one who welcomes from the altar, the cantor, the priest presiding, the one who proclaims the Word, those who present the gifts, the minister of the Eucharist, the choir, the sacristy team, those who organise the collection, those who clean the church, those who arrange the flowers.

The point of this variety is not just a division of labour, so many jobs to be done. The point is that the Eucharist mirrors the Christian community to itself. It is a ministering community. When we see somebody ministering during the Eucharist, it is not a functionary at a ceremony, still less an extension of a clerical caste. What we see is a living representation of what we are all meant to be.

This is perhaps most vividly expressed in the practice of ministers bringing the bread of life from the Eucharist to those at home. As they are sent, as they depart the church, we can see the bridge between 'liturgy here' and 'life out there'. We see ministry extend beyond the celebration. We see 'Mass' move into the mode of 'mission'. We see ourselves being sent.

Confirmation

This adds up to an imposing challenge. Where the Latin Mass said *Ite, missa est*, the familiar phrase today is, 'The Mass is ended; go in peace'; to which we reply, 'Thanks be to God.' The reply, however, can sound like, 'Thank God it's over!' Even when it does not, there's a sense of 'that's that – duty completed – done for another week'. Rather than, 'When the service is over, the real service begins'.

Which has comes first, Mass or mission? The idea is still strong that Mass is the main part of being a 'practising' Catholic – so that, when Mass is over, the main duty is done. But there is also a sense in which the Mass is a means to an end, rather than an end in itself.

The 'end' in question is that the paschal mystery, the power of life over death, would be a powerful force in our world and in our lives together. We celebrate this power in the Eucharist, but not in a complacent way, as if resting on our laurels. We do so in order to see our lives again from this point of view – and in order to live our lives more fully from this point of view.

I conclude by noting a correspondence between this 'sending' part of the Mass and the first 'gathering' part. The way we gather is meant to say something about who we are and how we see ourselves. It is meant to give expression to our baptismal identity. Gathering is meant to have a feel about it of being the body of Christ, called together through our baptism into the Body. We are meant to feel baptised.

In the same way, the sending is meant to say something about who we are as confirmed Christians. Confirmation means that we are each given a part to play in the church's task. It says that the church's mission is our shared undertaking in the power of the Spirit. The way we conclude should be an experience of being sent – an invitation and challenge to discover again our own Confirmation. We should go feeling confirmed.

B. PRACTICAL IDEAS FOR SENDING

(1)

After communion is the appropriate time to read announcements or notices. In many churches this is done at the end of the Liturgy of the Word. As one parish priest explained it, people who leave the church at communion would miss them if they were later in the Mass! But notices are already orienting us to the world outside; they belong at the stage when our minds are turning in that direction.

On this point, church notice boards and newsletters are the ordinary vehicle for communicating information. If this is in fact the case, announcements at the end of Mass can be very brief, confined to priority items and alerting people to further information to be found elsewhere.

Ideally announcements would revolve around matters to do with the mission of the parish. It is an appropriate time for parishioners (such as pastoral council members) to input about events or plans in the parish. Again, that would be putting in front of people something of the mission that all take with them from the Eucharist.

(2)

The following idea probably belongs after the homily, but is mentioned here because of its link with the theme of this part of the Mass. It is to have an occasional re-dedication of people involved in different ministries (or a commissioning in the case of people just starting).

Usually there is a commissioning of Ministers of Eucharist, but generally the potential in this kind of ritual is undervalued. The potential is twofold. On the one hand, it serves as an affirmation and a strengthening for those in the ministry. On the other, it heightens the consciousness of all present that all are called to ministry and mission.

The ritual itself can be quite simple – a word of introduction, a prayer, a symbolic action (e.g. Ministers of the Word take a bible in their hands while the priest says a blessing), followed possibly by a short creed and the prayers of the faithful.

Ministries connected with the Eucharist itself include: Ministers of the Eucharist and of the Word, singers and musicians, those in hospitality ministry, sacristy team, flowers group, church cleaners, servers, those who take care of the collections. As well, there are all the other ministries in the parish – baptism team, pastoral council, visitation team, bereavement group, youth group, finance/maintenance committee, and so on.

Some of these could be taken on their own, for instance the baptism team on the feast of Our Lord's Baptism. Others could be grouped together (for instance all those involved in the care of the church). The ideal might be that every weekend Mass experiences some such ritual occasionally. In that way there is an ongoing reminder of the confirmation call to ministry and mission that is the focus of the 'sending' part of the Mass.

(3)

At some Masses there is the practice of sending Ministers of the Eucharist with communion to people who are sick or housebound. As mentioned earlier, this is a powerful statement, at the end of Mass, of how we are all being sent forth.

Before the blessing, the ministers would come to the altar in a semi-circle while the priest says a prayer, before they each take a pyx from the altar and depart. The following is an example of the prayer that might be said:

> God our Father, we know that our communion in this Eucharist includes others who are not here with us, fellow members of the Body of Christ. We think especially of those who are sick or housebound in our parish family. We send

our ministers to them, to share the bread we have broken here. May this assure them that they belong to a community that cares about them.

(4)

Another option is to have a 'sending thought' before the blessing. This would be a very brief deliberate focusing of the whole congregation on their being sent. Something like this is probably needed, in order to focus people on seeing this point in the celebration as a beginning rather than just a conclusion. For instance, the following might be said, followed by just a moment's quiet before the blessing:[11]

This is the moment when we are sent with a mission …
Go from here to wherever life calls you.
Go – and take this Eucharist with you.
Take its blessing and bestow it;
take its grace and share it;
take its love and live it.

(5)

While the final song/hymn of the Mass will be on different themes on different occasions, it makes sense that it would frequently be a song on the theme of mission or ministry, again to reinforce the sense of being sent.

(6)

As part of the priest's blessing, it might be possible on some occasions to invite people to bless one another. Either before or after the priest gives the blessing, he could invite people to bless one person near them by signing the cross on their forehead.

If there was a small congregation this could be done blessing each other with water. Whatever way it is done, it would 'bring the blessing home' to people. It would give each one a stronger sense that they are blessed and calling to be a blessing for others.

(7)

Just as Mass begins with a procession, so should it end. And as the entrance procession unites us in a common gaze, all our eyes

11. See *Eucharist: Enhancing the Prayer* for more such texts.

drawn to the altar, so this procession to the door unites us in a common focus on reaching out with the good news of the gospel. A procession with liturgical movement can add to the meaning of the moment and accentuate the theme of being sent.

For the priest to kiss the altar, genuflect and head straight into the nearby sacristy sends out an entirely different message! Something like 'That's that and now we all go our separate ways; the business of this gathering is over.'

(8)

I spoke earlier about a welcoming ministry as people arrive at the church. This could be repeated as people leave. This time it would not be to welcome people, but to distribute a newsletter for instance, or some reflection/prayers based on today's celebration, or special leaflets on occasion. People tend to arrive at Mass all at once, so there is no space there for this kind of thing. But leaving is more leisurely.

At special times this ministry could take the form of a gift. For instance, presenting flowers on Mothers' Day, or sweets for the children on Easter Sunday. All this sends a message that we do not just 'head off', but that there is a spirit that binds us together as we disperse.

(9)

These little things – the priest meeting people as they leave, people distributing leaflets, etc. – are also saying that the end of Mass is a time for meeting and greeting, a time of conviviality. An extension of this is to have a cup of tea nearby after Mass. It is all part of working on the *human* feeling of community that makes the sense of community with God more tangible and real.

(10)

Maybe the time after Mass could also be used more often for mini-meetings, to make more of the time when people are gathered anyway, rather than their having to come out on a weeknight. By mini-meeting I mean people staying on or going to a nearby hall for fifteen minutes or so.

Examples of such meetings might be: to explain forthcoming elections for the pastoral council, or to give an update on a building project, or to present information about some new pastoral initiative in the parish. The business would be concluded promptly ; those who wish can stay on longer to chat over a cup of tea.

(11)
After Mass is also a suitable time for people to sign up for ministries or specific projects in the parish. There might be an annual 'Ministry Sunday', with a homily encouraging people in their giftedness, a handout listing possibilities, and somebody at a table outside to take names or give information.

There could be a similar process occasionally for specific needs. Indeed, there might well be a bigger response when what is requested is a once-off, short-term, manageable commitment to some very concrete project. Whichever it may be, these possibilities further build up the sense of the end of the Mass as a time of sending and mission.

Question for reflection/discussion
What do you think could be done that would best contribute
to people leaving Mass with an inspiring sense of being sent?